Ava Gardner

Touches of Venus

Ava Gardner

Touches of Venus

An Anthology

Gilbert L. Gigliotti
Editor

ENTASIS PRESS

WASHINGTON, D.C.

Published by
ENTASIS PRESS
Washington, D.C.
2010

ISBN 978-0-9800999-5-9

Library of Congress Control Number: 2009936474
Publisher: Entasis Press
Washington, D.C.

To my wife Martha

Iliad 24.537

Raymond Foye: Is there a poem you've yet to write?

John Wieners: I want to write a poem about an old person dying of loneliness. I want to write a poem about an old person, alone in a room, dying of hunger and loneliness. No one has ever written a poem about an old person dying in the cold, of hunger and loneliness. Except of course Ava Gardner, who is always our master.

John Wieners
Cultural Affairs in Boston, 1988

Contents

Introduction

"What She's Got You Couldn't Spell"

IN *THE BAREFOOT CONTESSA* (1954), there's a party scene at the Hollywood home of actress Maria Vargas, played by Ava Gardner, the spoken and unspoken object of every man's attention at the gathering. In front of Mr. and Mrs. Harry Dawes, Maria's director, the actress is accosted by an aging, drunken starlet, who finally slurs out:
"You haven't even got what I've got!"
Rising to Maria's defense, Mrs. Dawes responds:
"What she's got you couldn't spell, and what you've got, you used to have."

Ladies and gentlemen, I give you Ava Gardner.

Ava Gardner was a self-described hick from Grabtown, North Carolina, who was made a movie star by Hollywood in the clichéd way that, when we say "They don't make stars like they used to," we're absolutely correct; they don't.
In that way Ava Gardner was not unique. She was manufactured like so many others had been, and she struggled against the same powerlessness that all the smart ones did—wanting to grow as a person and actor while the studio system demanded much less and often necessitated against any such development. That, in both *One Touch of Venus* (1948) and The *Barefoot Contessa*, statues of Ava play prominent roles, and another was dedicated in 1998 in Tossa de Mar, Spain, the

shooting location of *Pandora and the Flying Dutchman* (1951), speaks volumes about our collective desire to capture her "Ava-ness" permanently.

While Ava started off her career with a screen test at which the director commented that, although she couldn't talk or act, he loved it anyway, and went on to make her share of forgettable films ("more than my share," she'd argue), she in fact grew on screen through a variety of important roles in classic films:

• Kitty Collins, the sultry temptress of *The Killers* with Burt Lancaster;

• the eponymous goddess in *One Touch of Venus* with Robert Walker;

• Julie LaVerne, the mulatta, in *Show Boat* with Howard Keel;

• Honey Bear Kelly in *Mogambo* with Clark Gable and Grace Kelly;

• Maria Vargas Torlato-Favrini in *The Barefoot Contessa* with Humphrey Bogart and Rossano Brazzi;

• Lady Brett Ashley in *The Sun Also Rises* with Tyrone Power and Errol Flynn;

• Moira Davidson in *On the Beach* with Gregory Peck and Fred Astaire;

• Eleanor Holbrook in *Seven Days in May* with Kirk Douglas and Burt Lancaster;

• alcoholic Maxine Davidson in *The Night of the Iguana* with Richard Burton and Deborah Kerr;

• matriarch Sarah in *The Bible* with George C. Scott;

• actress Lily Langtry in *The Life and Times of Judge Roy Bean* with Paul Newman;

• Remy Royce-Graff in *Earthquake* with Charlton Heston.

Not a bad run of movies and co-stars for someone who never considered herself much of an actress.

One of her greatest career disappointments lay in MGM's not using her recordings of "Can't Help Lovin' Dat Man" and "Bill" in *Show Boat* (1951) since the songs finally had given her the opportunity to use the natural southern drawl the studio had worked so hard to eradicate. And her roles in such films as *On the Beach* (1959), *Seven Days in May* (1963), and *The Night*

of the Iguana (1964) are remarkable in her apparent willing-
ness both to let go of her enduring inhibitions and to ignore
the life-long doubts about her talent. For she was a classic
beauty who, in the wake of a drunken bull-fighting accident
in 1958, learned to show her audience her age—often taking
roles that challenged us to see her stripped of any remnants of
Hollywood glamour. She channeled her life experiences—the
lust, the heartbreak, the impetuousness, the cynicism, and,
yes, the luck and the love—into creating characters who can
haunt us still.

She aged from hard living, hard loving, hard drinking,
and, along the way, became an international celebrity of the
highest order. She married actor Mickey Rooney, bandleader
Artie Shaw, and singer Frank Sinatra (who, while nary a good
husband among them, arguably comprise the most famous
hat trick of spouses ever amassed by a single actress). She was
a friend of writers Ernest Hemingway and Robert Graves. She
dated Howard Hughes, a whole bunch of actors, and even
bullfighters like Luis Miguel Dominguin and Mario Cabré,
one of her co-stars in *Pandora and the Flying Dutchman* and the
would-be poet and lover who authored the *Dietario Poético a
Ava Gardner*. Indeed, in the case of the *torero* Dominguin, it
was primarily their relationship that made him, at the time of
his death in 1996, worthy of widespread mention in American
obituaries—as no mere Hemingway story ever could.

After her third failed marriage, and caught by the exoticism
of Europe, she expatriated, living alone in Madrid and then
London for the final 35 years of her life, far from the North
Carolina hills—and even further from Hollywood, the place
she never could call home. Her embrace of the great big world
beyond show biz, and the globe's adoption of her in return,
in many ways separate her from all the other great Golden
Era actresses, and so the truly international dimension of this
anthology, with works from England, Ireland, Spain, France,
Greece, and New Zealand (with a nod to French Canada),
should come as no surprise. The comic routine of the Argen-
tinian musical troupe *Les Luthiers*, with its linguistic confusion
of "Ava Gardner" and "avant-garde," and a 1990 collection of
Hebrew poems by David Levin, entitled Ava Gardner Dead,

further testify to her international appeal.

This bare-bones biography, however, doesn't begin to explain the range of emotion and image on display in the following pages. The "Ava Gardner" of many of these writers of poetry, fiction, and non-fiction is beautiful, of course, but, as in Margaret Atwood's "Ava Gardner Reincarnated as a Magnolia," she's fiercely independent, outspoken, and not a little unpredictable. If she was superficial, she was deeply so (as she herself joked), but that awareness only added to the legacy of a woman who refused to just shut up and be beautiful ("Working at Pam-Pam's"). Robert Graves gives us a non-fiction portrait of a woman impatient of fame and eager to enrich her life with poetry.

She is an ideal ("Carrying a Torch"), a possibility ("Pandora"), an inspiration ("She Asked for a Joke or a Poem"), and a pun ("It's Not the Leaving of Wellington"). She fails at taming the wild Rooney ("Sitting with My Grandmother") but is reckoned a lifesaver ("The Swimming Teacher")—an oblique reference to her rescuing Sinatra personally and professionally when he was down-on-his-luck and his career seemed finished in the early 1950s. And it is Sinatra who appears in many of the poems and lyrics, since their affair, marriage, divorce, and ultimately lasting friendship represents one of the tragic love stories of the second half of the Twentieth Century—a passion, shared by both and recognized by all, that could survive neither their propinquity nor their personalities.

Ava and Frank's relationship inspired at least four of the six song lyrics included here: Vaughn's "Ava Gardner Blues," Russell's "When Sinatra Played Juarez," Vega's "Frank and Ava," and Berretta's "Frank and Ava's Child." Morgan's "Cold Coffee and Ava Gardner," like several other works including Owen's "Ava Gardner," highlights the powerful resemblance of a particularly significant woman (from lovers to mothers) to the striking actress, while the resemblance of "Cherry Darling" (Rose McGowan) to Ava, at least in eyes of "The Rapist" (Quentin Tarantino) takes an ugly turn in Robert Rodriguez's *Grindhouse* screenplay. French singer/songwriter Souchon's *"La Beauté d'Ava Gardner"* places her allure in a more metaphysical context—a symbol of the fleeting (yet irresistible!) grace of human experience.

Ava Gardner remains a challenge for us as well in these pages—with her vitality and her stupor, her love and her lust. If she is, in the end, a Venus, then she's divine in the way Homer's gods are so often, powerfully irresistible and wonderfully imperfect.

And I won't even mention the publicity for *The Barefoot Contessa* that billed Ava as "The World's Most Beautiful Animal!"

My thanks to my two lovely amanuenses/daughters, Cecilia and Celeste; the CCSU English Department secretary, Darlene Gable, for "do-doing that voo-doing" that she does so well on the computer; Moises Salinas; Antonio Garcia-Lozada; Melissa Mentzer; my publisher, Ed Perlman; Sara Ickow; Ravi Shankar; Kim Farrington, the entire Inter-Library Loan staff, and Joan Packer at the CCSU Elihu Burritt Library; Professor Peter Mackridge; biographer Lee Server; to the listeners of Frank, Gil, and Friends on WFCS 107.7 FM New Britain/Hartford.

Gilbert L. Gigliotti

Ava
Gardner
Touches of Venus

Robert Graves

from A Toast to Ava Gardner

WE HAD AN UNEXPECTED VISIT from Ava Gardner, a close friend of our Maryland friend Betty Sicre. Betty suggested that Ava should take a short holiday from the exhausting social life of Madrid to visit soporific and truly rural Majorca. There she could catch up on sleep, study Spanish grammar, swim daily, and consult me about how to finish her random education by a crash-course in English poetry. We had met Ava at Betty's house a few months before and found her great fun; afterwards she sent us a huge bouquet of red roses, an attention which my wife and I appreciated all the more because, as we already knew, Ava is not one to distribute idle favours. She was feeling lonely at this, her elder sister having just gone back to the States, and would borrow each of Betty's four small sons in turn to keep her company at night. "The other boys at the American School will think me a sissy," the youngest but one had tearfully complained, "if they find out that I sleep twice a week with Ava!"

At Palma's Son Bonet airport, she came rushing towards us across the tarmac: a startled deer, pursued by a hungry-looking wolf. When the wolf saw her suddenly engulfed in our large family—the children had played truant from school by telling their monks and nuns that an aunt was arriving from London—he slunk off slavering. But word flew from end to end of

1

the airport that the famous Ava Gardner had finally come to Majorca, and crowds went milling around In search of the red carpet, the bouquets, and the press photographers. Meanwhile, we hurried Ava into our Land-Rover, and hauled her baggage off the airline truck. One film-struck enthusiast saw a woman who closely resembled his idol bandying nonsense with our children in the dusty car; he stopped, narrowed his eyes, and passed on—it could not, of course, be she. We made a clean getaway.

Ava explained that there had been two really trouble-some Spanish wolves aboard the plane. The first, seated across the gangway, kept addressing her in an experi-mental sort of Italian, until she slammed shut the *Oxford Book of English Verse* (supplied by Betty for the poetry course) and said: "If you must interrupt my reading, why don't you at least talk your own language?"

The wolf answered gallantly: "Signorina, I decided to give myself the honour of employing your own musical tongue."

Ava looked puzzled. "You must have got things mixed," she said. "I happen to have married a Sicilian, but my Italian is even worse than yours."

The wolf leered at her craftily. "Do not think to de-ceive me! All our papers assure us that you are a true daughter of Naples." "

"Then they're lying. I was born and raised In North Carolina."

"A horrid doubt overtook the wolf. "Then I am mis-taken? You are not Sofia Loren?"

With a cry of indignation Ava leaped up and took refuge in a vacant seat forward, but found Wolf No.2 waiting there to pounce. So she read the *Oxford Book of English Verse* in the washroom, from which she emerged when the plane had landed; only to find the wolf waiting for her with amorous yelps at the foot of the landing-steps. Female film stars, it seems, are bound by a strict code: they must never insult journalists or press photographers, never refuse to sign autographs (unless desperately pressed for time), and never either slug wolves with overnight bags or poke out their eyes with parasols.

Ava's plans for improving her Spanish grammar and catching up on sleep did not come to much. There are too many places in Palma where gipsies strum at guitars and dance flamenco all night; and Ava can never resist flamenco. Besides, her first visit to Majorca attracted such immense attention that she was forced to change hotels four times in five days; but it fascinated us to bask for a while in the spotlight of her glory. Though far preferring, she said, a meal of shepherd's pie or sausage-and-mash at our Palma flat, she gallantly took us out once or twice to the lusher restaurants.

After dinner, in one of these, she asked me for her poetry lesson, and I told her that so few poems were worth reading, and so many were wrongly supposed to be worth reading, that she had better make sure she would not waste her time by this poetry course. Washing for gold could be very dull work. Then, changing the metaphor, I said that a clear, personal voice was better than all the technical skill and daring experimentation in the world—really good poetry always makes plain, immediate, personal sense, is never dull, and goes on making better sense the oftener one reads it. "Poems are like people," I said. "There are not many authentic ones around."

Questioned about the monstrous legendary self which towers above her, Ava told us that she does everything possible to get out from under, though the publicity-boys and the Press are always trying to clamp it even more tightly on her shoulders. Also, that she has never outgrown her early Hard-Shell Baptist conditioning on that North Carolina tobacco farm, with the eye of a wonderful father always on her; and still feels uncomfortably moral in most film-studios; it isn't what she does that has created her sultry reputation;

3

but what she says. Sometimes she just can't control her tongue.

A photographer suddenly let off a flash-bulb at us, and Ava flashed back at him almost as startlingly in the fiercest language. But when he apologized at once, she half forgave him. The rest of our talk was punctuated by the waiter's handing a succession of autograph-books to Ava for signature; she obliged automatically with a fixed, sunny smile, not losing the thread of our conversation until one autograph-hunter, an over-stuffed sofa of a woman, plumped herself down next to me, leant across me, and said: "Oh, dear Miss Gardner, *I have seen every single one* of your films! Now I wonder whether you would be so good as to give me your *personal* autograph, for my seven-year-old grandchild. Her name is Wendy Solgotch Wallinger."

Ava frowned. "Is the Solgotch Wallinger strictly necessary?" she asked. "And what am I supposed to write on?"

"Oh, I thought film stars always supply the paper!"

Ava frowned more deeply. Her comments on that paper shortage had better stay off record. They were quite enough to account for her sultry reputation. Nevertheless, loth to infringe the code further, she tore a corner off the menu, scribbled "Wendy, with best wishes from Ava Gardner," and waved Mrs. Wallinger away with it.

Having found my *Collected Poems* at our apartment, Ava asked which of them to read first. This question embarrassed me, after what I had already told her. However, there was one, I said, which she might perhaps like to take personally; though it had been written long before we met. I marked the page for study when she went to bed that night—if she ever did:

4

She speaks always in her own voice
Even to strangers...

and:

She is wild and innocent, pledged to love
Through all disaster...

That was Ava to the life.

Mario Cabré

You Don't Understand Me

El decir más diverso de los mares
no es jamás extranjero entre las playas.
Conferencian ensueños con estrellas,
y rocíos discurren con mañanas.

> You don't understand me.
> I don't understand you.

Rosa o fuente, palmera o amatista,
comprenden el gorjeo de los pájaros;
y conversan los montes y las nubes
acaso con un eco milenario.

> You don't understand me.
> I don't understand you.

Habla el niño a los senos de la madre
con el robusto verbo del instinto,
y responde la carne aprisionada
con el dulce lenguaje del latido.

> You don't understand me.
> I don't understand you.

La rotunda tristeza de la lluvia
dialoga a su vez con la añoranza
El río va dejando en al paisaje
la traducción del tiempo que se escapa.

> You don't understand me.
> I don't understand you.

Las amorosas manos de las ramas
con la constancia insomne de la tierra,
descifran uno a uno los mensajes
de los distintos aires cuando llegan.

You don't understand me.
I don't understand you.

Los siglos martillean en las piedras
con las palabras que entienden las auroras,
¡Qué intercambio de voces tiene el alma
con la expresión interna de las cosas!

You don't understand me.
I don't understand you.

S'Agaró, 1.⁰ de mayo
(Lunes, noche)

Mario Cabré

You Don't Understand Me

translated by Katherine Sugg

The most various voice of the sea
Is never a stranger to the shore.
Dreams confer with stars,
And dewdrops speak to mornings.

> You don't understand me.
> I don't understand you.

Flower or fountain, palm tree or amethyst,
They understand the calling birds;
And mountains converse with clouds,
Echoing through the ages.

> You don't understand me.
> I don't understand you.

The baby talks to his mother's breast
Robust act of instinct,
And the flesh responds imprisoned
In the sweet idiom of a heartbeat.

> You don't understand me.
> I don't understand you.

The full sadness of the rain
Speaks in turn to nostalgia
The river lowers into the landscape
Carving a translation of time gone by.

> You don't understand me.
> I don't understand you.

The passionate hands of trees
With the wakeful persistence of the earth,
Decipher one by one the messages
Of each breeze as it arrives.

You don't understand me.
I don't understand you.

The centuries hammer into the rocks
Words heard by the dawn.
Such exchanges has the soul
With the secret meaning of things!

You don't understand me.
I don't understand you.

S'Agaró, May 1st.
(Monday, night).

Clive Fencott

Becoming a Servant to the Stars

THE MONEY SUPPLY was erratic. Particularly in the summer months when the colleges and schools were closed. I got round this by joining an unorthodox employment agency doing jobs for the rich and famous and not necessarily either. You could work when you wanted and as often as you wanted. This usually meant being a char-person in posh houses in and around Chelsea and Kensington. I was Ava Gardner's odd job man for a few weeks. One of my responsibilities being to put her record collection—mainly Frank Sinatra—in alphabetical order.

For some time I worked in a select little hotel in Kensington where film stars were wont to stay when in town working. I had a job as a room service waiter and had many invigorating conversations with the stars.

"Can I get you anything?", I enquired.
"No thank you," Peter Lorre replied.

"Is there anything else?", I enquired.
"No thank you," replied Katharine Ross.

"Is there something wrong?", I enquired.
"Yes! Where is the salt," demanded Shelley Duvall.

Scatman Crothers also stayed at the hotel while he was filming part of *The Shining* with Jack Nicholson. He was full of stories and would get out his tenor ukulele at the drop of a hat and sing old comic songs such as "Some of My Best Friends Are Shoes."

Alton Rivers

from Love, Ava

SUDDENLY FROM ACROSS THE ROOM came the sound of breaking glass. He looked in the direction the noise had come from, and though her back was toward him, he instantly recognized the black strapless dress and her dark hair. It was Ava. A broken vase lay on the floor beside the stereo, apparently knocked off when she raised the top of the cabinet to play a record. Now, as she fumbled with the sound system's controls, there was the loud, unnerving sound of the needle scratching across a record. A second attempt, and then Spanish music filled the room.

She turned, kicked off her shoes, and strode toward the center of the room, bare arms raised, fingers working as if playing castanets. She began dancing in small, precise steps to the flamenco guitar, her hips moving rhythmically, an arrogant set to her head and shoulders, the overall effect a brazen, natural sexiness. Her eyes held Russ's.

The crowd clapped in time to the music, and she extended her arms toward an older man with a gray goatee, inviting him to dance with her. He politely refused, blushing. She turned to the Iraqi general, demanding that he dance with her, and when he, too, declined she took a defiant stance, feet set wide apart, hands on her hips. "What's wrong with everyone?" She tossed her head and her eyes flashed dangerously. "Am I not cultured enough for you bastards?"

A swarthy man stepped forward, preparing to join her.

"No, no, no!" she cried scornfully, moving away from him. "I'll choose who I dance with, goddamn it!" Once again her eyes gazed steadily into Russ's.

She was obviously drunk, yet her steps and words were precise, unimpaired.

Russ watched and waited. "There she goes," said the man standing next to him. "She's wonderful until it gets dark and there've been too many martinis. And then it's Ava from hell."

She danced forward, her hips swaying to the music. "Such a *wonderful* group of men," she mocked. "All of this power and money, and all so goddamned *civilized*. Not one of you could hold your own against the poorest Gypsy in all of goddamned Spain!" She took a glass from a man, drank its murky contents, then threw it against the wall and resumed dancing.

Several guests prepared to leave, whispering as they made their way to the door. She watched them, an arched eyebrow and a sarcastic laugh her only reaction.

"Let's go to the bars, Ava!" shouted a man in the group surrounding her.

She stopped dancing. "Yes, let's do. We'll race our cars to Soho. Dance all night."

She turned to a young man with tanned skin and long hair, his open silk shirt revealing strands of gold chains. She grabbed his arm and said, "I'll take you." Then she turned to another older man. "And you."

She strode on, scanning the men at the bar. "It's going to be a *wonderful* night of bar crawling and dancing, but *not* with you...or you...or you," she said, pointing to one man after another. Then her eyes returned to Russ and she stopped in front of him.

"And I had thought the climax...the end of this evening would be just us," she said in a low, provocative voice. "I thought...a fun romp...just the two of us. So handsome and irresistible, but I saw you with that woman." She tossed her head and laughed contemptuously. Then, her voice back to normal, she said, "Stay here, Major, with your fat blonde."

"Come, Ava," implored the tanned man with the gold chains.

"Yes, let's go," she said, laughing, and joined the others. Noisily they were out the door and into the night.

Everyone stood motionless, only exchanging glances. It was as if no one knew what to do in the aftermath of the storm. There was an empty, breathless depression, a vacuum in the sudden absence of noise and movement and energy.

Jim Harrison

from Ghazals

X.

Praise me at Durkheim Fair where I've never been, hurling
grenade wursts at those who killed my uncle back in 1944.

Nothing is forgiven. The hurt child is thirty-one years old
and the girl in the pale blue dress walks out with another.

Where love lies. In the crawl space under the back porch
thinking of the aunt seen shedding her black bathing suit.

That girl was rended by the rapist. I'll send her a healing
sonnet in heaven. Forgive us. Forgive us. Forgive us.

The moon I saw through her legs beneath the cherry tree had
no footprints on it and a thigh easily blocked out its light.

Lauren Hutton has replaced Norma Jean, Ava Gardner, Lee Remick
and Vanessa Redgrave in my Calvinist fantasies. Don't go away.

John Williams

Carrying a Torch
(The Usher's Song)

I remember when old movies meant they were made before my time,
bright with stars of yesteryear when a dime was worth a dime.
Now I watch the late night shows I first saw in my teens,
when women pulled on cigarettes and only men wore jeans.

Lady lady shine your light make a grey world black and white,
I've grown old like faded celluloid,
I've reeled from reel to reels
watching spinning stagecoach wheels
and John Wayne winning wars on land and sea.

I remember when the heroes were something to be seen,
but it's hard to be heroic trapped inside a twelve inch screen,
Jimmy Dean was such a giant he was born to grow and grow,
but they put him on the tee-vee and the adman stole the show.

Lady lady shine your light make a grey world black and white,
I've grown old like faded celluloid,
I've reeled from reel to reels
watching spinning stagecoach wheels
and John Wayne winning wars on land and sea.

I remember when a love scene meant you never saw at all,
but now the skin is sprayed on, and it stretches wall to wall,
I still love Ava Gardner and her sea-green bedroom eyes,
that's all I ever knew of her apart from off-screen sighs.

Margaret Meyers

Leaving Johnston County

I'M RUMMAGING THROUGH A PILE of mangoes at the market so I don't notice him right away. I'm in avid pursuit of perfectly ripe mangoes with sunset skin, all yellow, pink and orange. Not that perfection is necessary when you're just making a pie, but lately I need distractions.

"I assume you've heard the news," he says mildly. "Should you be out and about by yourself?"

Beside me stands a great white hunter type straight out of *Mogambo*—except that he's too handsome to be Clark Gable. Built long and lean, he has classic Irish good looks: blue-black hair, dark blue eyes, deeply cleft chin. He looks better in khaki than any man I've ever seen. When I catch myself wishing I'd worn something more feminine than faded blue pedal pushers and a plain white blouse, even the freckles on the backs of my knees redden with shame. As they should, especially under the circumstances. "If you mean do I know the rebels are marching on Coquilhatville, yes I do," I say briskly. "But Coq is at least eight hundred kilometers away from Leopoldville. And one still has to eat."

Leopoldville is overrun with white soldiers of fortune from Rhodesia and South Africa just now, and I'm guessing he's one of them.

"I'm walking you home," he says, and stands patiently aside until I have purchased the fruit. Then he takes my string

17

bag of mangoes and offers me his left arm with gently mocking gallantry. I can just imagine what the Hansens would say if I took it.

"It's three kilometers," I warn him, but he is not deterred. Seized by an unfamiliar recklessness, I accept his escort, if not his arm, and we head down the dusty side street overhung with Nandi flame trees. By the end of the first kilometer, I know all about his mother's asthma, the heavily mortgaged family farm, his sister Nancy's favorite spaniel Patmore. By the end of the second kilometer he knows all about my darling Bill and how I met him at a Youth for Christ rally in Richmond. He knows about the family in North Carolina too, and my secretarial course at Atlantic Christian College. After the third kilometer he knows that my five-and-a-half-year-old Amy is reading already, that I miss Hershey's chocolate syrup and Almond Joys, even that I sneak off to the American Embassy's open-to-the-public movie nights. If there had been a fourth kilometer, Lord knows what he might have found out—maybe my brand of deodorant?

He walks me to the door of our small cinder-block house just inside the gated enclave of the Evangelical Community Mission Society of Congo. He's in the middle of saying he hopes he'll see me before he's posted east when Ava is back again, whispering throatily in my ear: *Well, darling, that man's a charmer! Easily the finest looking hunk of mercenary I've ever seen.*

While I squeeze fresh limes, I gaze out the kitchen window at my daughter and her *mobatelii*, Mama Marta, sitting in the shade of the breadfruit tree. Mama Marta is twisting Amy's fine blond locks into myriad little spikes stiffened with rough black thread while she hums a jazzy fragment of song from Radio Leopoldville. She pauses, studies the drooping spikes covering my daughter's head, then shakes her head. "White people hair is just *mpamba*, useless," she says. She holds a pocket mirror to Amy's face and both of them burst out laughing. It's hard now to remember that I hadn't wanted a nanny; I'd thought it colonial, this business of white missionaries handing over their children to be cared for by Congolese. But the day Mama Marta came round to offer her services, I looked at the wide, kind eyes above deeply scarified cheekbones and changed my mind. Now Mama Marta comes every afternoon from one to five. In these uncertain days her dependability is especially reassuring—although I do send her home early so she won't be caught outdoors after curfew.

I carry two glasses of limeade to the back yard. As I hand one to Mama Marta she says, "Listen, about the man who walked you back from the *marché* just now. He wasn't one of *them*, was he?"

By *them* Mama Marta means *les affreux*, the frightful ones, which is a popular nickname for the white mercenaries Presiden Kasavubu has hired to help the Congolese National Army put down the rebellion in the eastern part of the country. Mama Marta is one of the many Congolese who are livid with Kasavubu for paying white men from white supremacist countries to fight his own people. And it's not only the Congolese who are furious: African leaders all over the continent have denounced his action.

"Yes," I say. "Yes, he was, but he seemed like a nice man anyway."

"Nice! Listen, these *affreux* ignore curfew, get into drunken brawls in the *cité*, womanize—and worse. Much worse. Really, I think this terrible *crise* is getting to be too much for you."

I'm inclined to be indignant and ask why it should be harder for me than anyone else. I like to think I'm not faint of heart, and certainly I believe that most of us, however sincere, are as much adventurers as missionaries. But I don't want to hear her answer so I let my indignation go.

"You see, you just aren't used to hardships like we are," she says. "We're always *en crise* here, even in times of peace. There's poverty, for one thing. And food shortage, cholera outbreaks, rogue leopards and elephants."

I remember that moment in *Mogambo* when Ava Gardner, fed up with East Africa and her great white hunter, says the only lions she ever wants to see again are the two in front of

19

the public library.

Three months ago the American Embassy showed *Mogambo* on movie night. I was dying to go, as I'd never seen it before. Bill agreed to watch Amy and say I was lying down with a migraine if any of our missionary colleagues, particularly the nosy Reverend and Mrs. Hansen, happened to drop by. Bill is amused by what he calls the HASR, the Helen and Ava Special Relationship. He knows both of us were farm girls from Johnston County, North Carolina, both of us had conservative religious upbringings, both of us attended Atlantic Christian College, and he says he's fine with the HASR as long as I don't leave him for Hollywood. And as long as our missionary colleagues don't find out that I watch her movies whenever I get the chance. Movies are secular, which is bad enough, but movies starring an adulterous, boozing, swearing female are out of the question and a TME, a Terrible Moral Example. (I love the man, but his acronyms get old after a while.)

On that night the rebellion in the east still seemed a small, easily containable matter, and there was no curfew yet. I made a production of getting dressed while Bill lounged on the bed and watched. I put on my favorite white blouse, a blue-striped seersucker skirt and a wide white belt, and dabbed a little Yardley's English Rose cologne on my wrists and throat. I knew Ava wore a fabulously expensive rose scent made by Creed in 1948 just for her. According to one of my magazine clippings (Jean is so good about mailing me anything Ava-related) the "elegantly named *Fleur de Thé Rose Bulgare* is lightened by lemon, bergamot, and green tea," which I find surprising. I'd have expected Ava to prefer a more sultry rose, a rose laden with amber, sandalwood, maybe a little jasmine.

Bill drove me to the gymnasium the embassy frequently rented for big public film events. After warning me to choose my late-evening taxi driver with care, he gave me a lovely, hard kiss and drove off. I found a prime seat on one of the lower bleachers next to two elderly white men whom I recognized as a much-fêted team of American ethnomusicologists who'd been spending a semester at the Louvainium. On my other side a young Congolese man in a dark suit talked quietly with a woman wearing a traditional *liputa* and a lacy white blouse. Once the movie began, my seatmates kept up a running commentary.

"How do these Brits get away with punishing Kenyans for poaching on their own land?" the Congolese man wanted to know.

"War drums, my eye," grumbled one of the ethnomusicologists. "If that's not a call to bring food and drink for a party, I'll eat my hat."

"What are these Wagenia tribesmen doing tracking the gorillas of east Congo anyway?" the Congolese woman asked her escort. "Aren't they river people? Fishermen?"

Me, I wondered why the director thought Africans should roll their eyes wildly all the time, but I kept the question to myself. At eleven years old, *Mogambo* was already a colonial period piece only too easy to ridicule. I just wanted to enjoy Ava, especially Ava in GEA, Glamorous East Africa. I had a 1953 magazine article with photos of Ava at Nairobi's New Stanley Hotel during the filming. She wore a white linen dress with a beautiful drape, a pale yellow cardigan, and a single string of pearls. In one photo she stood in the New Stanley's courtyard café reading the famous thorn tree, which functioned as a community message board—generally messages like "Soldier of fortune available immediately. Write to P.O. Box 2253 in Mombasa." Or "Guide needed for trek to Somali border in September. Must be crack shot. Danger pay." If Ava herself put up a message, what might it say? "Wanted: replacement for Frank Sinatra. Great white hunters welcome. Mercenaries welcome. No missionaries, please."

Although *Mogambo* was a wonderful showcase for Ava's beauty (how that emerald green sweater showed off the red highlights in her hair, and how the white one framed her perfect shoulders!) the movie really celebrated her extravagant, neck-or-nothing, kick-the-furniture nature. She raged; she provoked; she confronted; she lusted; she savored; she

21

rejoiced. I considered the quietness of my days. On Mondays, Wednesdays and Fridays I taught sewing, reading and writing to Congolese girls. On Tuesdays, Thursdays and Saturdays I dealt with housekeeping chores: I cleaned, did the laundry, boiled drinking water, ground peanuts for peanut butter, made mango-pineapple chutney to disguise the taste of Spam. Ava's Africa was cocktails-on-safari Africa; mine was worrying my colleagues might catch me watching her on an embassy film night. And it was on that night that I first heard Ava's voice.

After adding the tiniest drop of almond flavoring, I pour the mango pie filling into the prepared crust. My mother would make a lattice top crust but I content myself with a sprinkling of streusel. I listen to the BBC, hoping for an update; in this I am like everyone else in Leopoldville, including President Kasavubu and his military advisors. If the BBC doesn't know what's going on, then nobody does.

A soft ko-ko-ko announces Mrs. Hansen at the front door, wearing an expression of doleful sympathy, one of her omnipresent lace-edged hankies tucked into her belt. Smiling brightly, I let her in. Coffee? Something cold? Mrs. Hansen, sighing heavily, says she only wishes she knew what on earth to say to me, then asks how I am holding up. I say I am resting in His promises, and do come into the living room and sit down.

Mrs. Hansen asks about my sewing classes, and I tell her the girls are showing real proficiency with the satin stitch. At the very edge of my mind I hear Ava: *Satin stitch? At a time like this you're teaching a bunch of girls to SATIN STITCH? Holy shit, you've got to be kidding!*

Mrs. Hansen fidgets a little, smoothes her drip-dry Dacron-cotton skirt over her bumpy knees. The late afternoon sun floods through the living room window, making bold orange patterns on the bare, concrete floor. When Mrs. Hansen crosses her legs, one sandaled foot tangles with the sunlight and seems to catch fire.

"The State Department families have left, and so have most

of the other missionaries," she says. "Even those Evangelical Free Church folk from upcountry who thrive on adversity have left. Reverend Hansen is thinking it might be wise to reserve seats on the Thursday evening flight to Brussels."

The woman actually calls her own husband Reverend? How much do you bet that when they're having sex she says "Hey Reverend, move your fingers a little to the left—a little more—yes, that's it, Reverend. You've got it, Reverend! Oh, praise the Lord!"

In my mind I tell Ava she's got to behave herself, but of course I don't mean it. Ava has become my favorite distraction.

Amy pops her head around the doorframe to announce that Mama Marta has left extra early tonight. "The rebels don't worry her," Amy tells us. "But she's upset about *les affreux*. She says they do terrible, horrible things to African ladies. Can we read *Paddington Bear*?"

Mrs. Hansen and I exchange glances. "Well, if there's anything the Reverend and I can do," she says, getting to her feet.

As I see her to the door, I'm thinking that Ava's Africa, the cocktails-on-safari Africa, has a lot of appeal. I've never had a cocktail. Never tried liquor at all, in fact. Right now I'd like to.

My devout parents were thrilled when Bill and I decided to be missionaries to Congo. Our church was known to have a BFM (Burden for Missions) but had yet to send out any of their own church members to Africa. Bill felt a bit guilty about all the approval coming our way because of this decision.

"If I'm honest," Bill had said, "being a missionary is as much an adventure as a calling. I don't want to live in Johnston County all my life. I'd like to see the other side of the world, and maybe do something moderately useful while I'm at it."

Twenty-odd years ago Ava Gardner hadn't wanted to spend her life in Johnston County either. As far as I know she never regretted exchanging the tobacco farm for Hollywood—though she didn't enjoy acting all that much. But she did love acting out. She always had. The Gilmores, distant relatives of my mother who attended the same church as the Gardner family, told us that the teenaged Ava often went to services at a nearby Pentecostal church and was frank about why: "It's so exciting to gabble in tongues. You get to wave your hands in the air and scream and cry for the fun of it instead of sitting quietly in a pew agonizing over your sins and repenting." I could understand that; sometimes I wanted to scream my feelings to the world, my joys, my sorrows, but it just wasn't possible. Even when I was giving birth to Amy at a European clinic in Leopoldville I labored in a grim, panting silence. The Italian nursing sisters chattered, shouted, laughed, wept, cheered, and so did the Italian doctor, who confessed he'd had a few glasses of wine. (A few bottles, more like, Bill said later, and thank God you didn't need the episiotomy after all.) One of the nursing sisters said I didn't have to be so *stoico*, and I didn't know how to tell her that this was just me, true daughter of my mother. This was how things were done down my way in Johnston County, North Carolina. Unless you were Ava Gardner.

"Listen, I worry for you." Mama Marta sits on a chair in the kitchen with Amy slumped against her sturdy torso taking her afternoon nap. She is watching me spray ant killer in the freshly-scrubbed cupboards. "The army ants—if they want to come, they'll come. Remember last time when they ate all your *mondele* poison along with everything else in the house?"

I do. They were unfazed.

"You might as well just take a rest, Madame Helen."

I tell her one more time that I don't like being called Madame. "It's for colonials, that kind of title. For the Belgians. Congo's been independent for four years, and I'm American. Can't you call me just plain Helen?"

Mama Marta laughs silently, exposing front teeth carefully chiseled to fine points for beautification purposes. "But then you'd want to call me just plain Marta, and that wouldn't be respectful of my old age, would it? I would no longer feel entitled to give you advice."

"Oh, but I need your advice and I respect your age," I say. "And I like to call you Mama Marta. I feel you are my *mobateli* as much as Amy's."

Mama Marta leans her cheek against Amy's hair, which is still tied up in wilting spikes. "Then I would advise you not to speak with *les affreux*. You don't know what they might do, these white men who come from white-run African countries."

She's right. I know this, but just as I open my mouth, Amy, lifting her head from Mama Marta's capacious bosom, forestalls me.

"Mama Marta says that if people ask I must tell them that you are a *missionaire*, not a *mercenaire*. They are different and I must pronounce them carefully or people might get confused."

I stare at my daughter, at Mama Marta. "Of course they are different!" I say. "*Nakamwi.*"

Mama Marta stands Amy on her feet and says she must head home before it gets dark and the Congolese National Army starts patrolling the streets and arresting curfew-breakers.

Curfew, Ava snaps. *I'll give them curfew. No one's keeping me in if I want to go out, goddammit.*

I put Amy to bed. I spray more ant spray. I try to tune in to the BBC but all I get is a lot of static and eventually Radio South Africa, where some crooner with an Afrikaaner accent is pretending to be Bing Crosby. After I polish all the shoes in the house, I check on Amy again. She's sound asleep and breathing heavily. I crawl in beside her. I curve around her close as mango skin to mango flesh.

I've mended everything in the house that needed mending. I've made a new batch of Bill's favorite tangerine marmalade. I've written my parents and Bill's parents yet another no-news-yet-but-we're-all-hopeful letter on airmail paper the color of blue hydrangeas. Amy is chanting some made-up rhyme as she plays jump rope in the driveway with little

Rosie Hansen from next door. When I realize she is saying "Kasavubu made a boo-boo," even the hairs on my arms stand on end. I run out the front door to tell her this rhyme is not a good idea. Before I can open my mouth, I see my handsome mercenary standing several yards away, slapping his knees and laughing.

"It's not funny, Mr. Mercenary," I hiss at him. "Did you put them up to this?"

"The name's Ronan, remember?" he says, blue eyes crinkling disarmingly. "And why would I put them up to anything? I'm on Kasavubu's side. I think he's a basically good man, to tell you the truth, though I could wish he had a little more charisma and savvy."

"Me too," I say ruefully. Kasavubu just doesn't measure up to the martyred Patrice Lumumba, who is a national hero and the patron saint of the Congo's rebel army even though he's been dead for three years.

Amy slips her hand in mine and says in a stage whisper, "Does he have news about Daddy? About when he's coming back?"

"No, sweetheart." I squeeze her hand. "I think he just came to say hello and goodbye. He's going east to Stanleyville."

"So he's a mercenary then. Will he kill rebels?"

Kill is a nasty word. I wish Amy didn't know it. Little farm girls in North Carolina do, but generally "kill" applies to chickens and pigs.

"As a matter of fact, I do have news about your Daddy," Ronan tells her gently, then looks at me. "Really good news."

I crush Amy's hand till she squeals. I try to speak, but no words come. My heartbeats ring in my ears.

"He's about fifty kilometers from Lisala," Ronan says. "I made ham radio contact with some friends of mine upriver, and they did a little scouting around and found a Bill Forrester at the Bolala Mennonite Mission. They figured there couldn't be more than one Bill Forrester, so they got him a seat on a bush plane to Leopoldville tomorrow."

"*What* bush plane," I want to know. "There haven't been

any flights for weeks."

"We've got our own network. O'Halloran has a friend who owes him and happens to fly a little Cessna as well as run a cocoa plantation in the Ubangi. And O'Halloran owes me."

Amy pulls her hand away and says well, that's nice, because Paddington Bear was beginning to miss him. Then she and Rosie start to jump rope again. "Kasavubu made a boo-boo. Kasavabu made a boo-boo."

I start to shush them but Ava interrupts: *Don't rain on their parade, sweetheart. Let the kids enjoy themselves. They're just kids, for fuck's sake.*

Ronan stares at me, an eyebrow raised, and I stare back in befuddled horror. Did Ava say that or did I?

"Apparently when Bill learned that commercial flights and boats were cancelled and the rebels were coming west, he hitchhiked east of the city to Bolala Mennonite Mission. He remembered they had an airstrip and hoped against hope that someone—anyone—would use it at some point."

I had told Bill he shouldn't take that trip. Told him again and again. "Things are too uncertain," I had said—and Bill, foolhardy optimist that he is, just told me that I worried too much. "Everyone knows the rebels are too disorganized and too high on hemp and *kisi* to get very far."

"There was a missionary named Fred Klassen at Bolala as well," Ronan says. "Some agronomist who initially planned to protect his experimental poultry farm from hungry rebels. Not very practical thinking for a pacifist who doesn't know which end of a gun the ammo comes out of. Fred will be on that plane as well."

"He can stay with us, of course," I say calmly. "We've no proper guest room, but I'll make up the camp cot in the living room."

"I doubt the lack of a proper guest room will weigh heavily with him just now," Ronan says with just the shadow of a sideways grin.

I gaze at him. My hero. Clark Gable after all. Rescuer of my darling, idiotic, infuriating, moronic Bill...Oh, better than Clark Gable!

"You've been more than kind," I say primly. Do I sound appreciative enough? I worry I don't. I worry that I sound like my mother when she's trying to end a conversation with someone she dislikes. And I am appreciative. It's just that words, the right words, hang thoroughly out of my reach—just like the best mangoes. "Much more than kind."

"Wish me luck," he says.

"I do," I assure him earnestly. "And I hope this job pays off that mortgage."

We shake hands. His hand is hard and warm. He turns abruptly and heads back toward Avenue Eisenhower. As I watch him disappear into the late-afternoon shadows of the Nandi flame trees, Ava says: *Well, that was pretty damn cold of you, wasn't it? Why didn't you at least hug the man, for God's sake? Don't you think he deserves it? The State Department can't find out anything for twenty-six days, and he locates your lost Bill in—what—forty-eight hours?*

I tell Ava I'm sorry, really I am, but kind and helpful mercenaries haven't exactly come my way before.

Don't sound so morally superior. You do realize you have a lot in common, don't you? Mercenaries kill people for money, missionaries kill cultures for God. Any old way you look at it, it's murder. Ask yourself why on earth young Congolese women should take up embroidery, the Victorian opiate of western womanhood?

"You never thought up that line on your own, Ava," I say.

No, Artie Shaw said something like that once, and I liked it. But don't try to change the subject. I suppose you've taught them the daisy chain and the feather stitch as well?

"Listen, that's not all I do. I teach girls to read and write. Also older women who might never get the chance. And so does Bill. That's why he was up at Lisala in the first place; he was running pedagogy classes for new teachers."

Stick with that, then, and be humble about it. As for foisting the satin stitch on people, my domestic science teacher did that to me too—but that was Johnston County. And we don't have to live there any more, do we? DO WE?

What turmoil: Bill will be home, Mercenary Angel Ronan is heading east, and Ava—Ava is mad at me.

"Madame Helen, I think I am hearing good news about your man?" Mama Marta appears beside me, arms folded but her lips parted in a broad smile. "Is this true?"

I tell her yes, it's true.

"I like being surprised by goodness," she says.

Amy rushes over to Mama Marta and tells her Daddy is coming home tomorrow, but she always knew he would. She didn't worry about him one little bit; she just did lots of things—jump-roped, shelled peanuts for peanut butter, read books, got her hair done, stayed busy. Like Mama.

"That's right, sweetheart, worrying is always a waste of time and energy," I tell her. "Anyway, God was watching over him."

Oh, give it a rest. God's cutest mercenary was watching over him, and listen—don't look so guilty. I know you love your Bill, but we all have these little attractions.

I snap awake as something first tickles my skin and then sets it on fire. I fumble for the switch on the bedside table lamp. (Rebellions aren't nearly as bad as they could be as long as the electricity is still working.) A two-inch-thick column of army ants is marching across my bare left leg, just a few of the ants pausing now and then to sink their pincers into my flesh. To my right another column marches steadily across the yellow flowered sheet toward my pillow. There will be more, of course, marching relentlessly through the living room, the dining room, the kitchen, the bathroom. We must find shelter elsewhere. Maybe the Hansens next door? But she fusses so; we'll be up all night while she commiserates: "Army ants, on top of everything else, oh poor dear Helen." The mission vehicle, a battered green Ford pickup with a squeaky fan belt, would be better. It's parked in our drive and I have

Bill's key.

The ants haven't made it to Amy's room yet, and she is sound asleep, her lashes long upon her sunburned cheeks. She's clutching her quilt, smiling. I scoop her up in my arms, quilt and all, and carry her out the front door and crunch across the gravel to the pickup. Amy gurgles faintly when she sinks into worn upholstery smelling of Congolese rainy-season mold, and pokes her thumb into her mouth. I tuck the quilt around her, unroll the passenger window several inches, shut the door as quietly as I can, and hurry back inside the house.

Now there are several thick ant columns marching down the brightly lit hallway into the kitchen. I squat down on the bare concrete floor and stare at the invasion up close, particularly the oversized heads of those ants with the biggest, sharpest pincers who seem to police the maneuvers and keep the borders tidy. What dense, frenetic order. What apparent purpose. Where do they come from? Where do they go after they've alarmed everyone, displaced them, and polished every square inch of the house with formic acid?

I kneel down in the hallway just a few inches from the ants and grasp a section of the hem of my nightgown in my hands. Carefully, gingerly, I dip the section of the hem into the ants' scurrying stream. Most of the ants march onward, impervious, but the dozen or so who permit themselves to be distracted lock their pincers into the soft cotton knit and hang on for dear life. I withdraw my hem and briefly admire the neat row of dangling insects. How richly they glisten in the light; I didn't expect to be reminded of sheeny dark-gold droplets of molasses. Then, one by one, I pinch the bodies off, leaving the disproportionately large heads ferociously gripping the fabric.

The effect is subtly decorative, like a trimming of little tiny brown beads. I put every single inch of hemline through this process, at one point hastily taking off my nightgown then putting it on again, back to front.

Wish I'd thought of that on the Mogambo set. Clark would've loved it. Now, how about a little celebration? A little singing, laughing, that sort of thing. You know what that old saint said—Frank told me about him but I forget his name—"Laugh and grow stong."

"Ignatius. Saint Ignatius. I don't know why I know that when I'm from Johnston County. Protestant country, as you know."

Johnston County had one good thing I took full advantage of. You remember that fabulous Holy Roller church? How about a little shouting, a little speaking in tongues? What songs do you know?

"What a Friend We Have in Jesus?"

Oh, I know that one. Come on, let's sing it. Dance it. You should try swishing that hemline nearer your thighs than your knees, for once. You have the legs for it.

And so I do. I swish swish swish as I sing louder than I've ever done in my life:

"Yesu ndeko na bolingo, ngai nalingi yo mingi."

Lordy, Helen, what on earth is that? Are you speaking in tongues already? I don't know those words.

I realize I'm singing in Lingala. For five years I have only sung this song in Lingala, and the English escapes me. Just as the English now escapes me for Victorian gems like "The Holly and the Ivy" and "In the Bleak Midwinter," both of them translation problems since there's no Lingala word for holly, ivy, or snow. Are hymns another satin stitch export?

No, don't stop. Keep on singing whatever it is you're singing. It's fabulous. Just a slightly faster tempo, maybe?

I say let's start over. Ready? "Yesu ndeko na bolingo, ngai nalingi yo mingi!"

What a friend we have in Jesus, all our sins and griefs to bear!—You've got it, girl. You're on a roll, and don't hold back. That is some ass-kicking vibrato! Oh, sweet Jesus. Sweet, sweet Jesus.

I don't hold back. After a few minutes, Amy wanders sleepily in the front door and takes my hand. She says oh, wow, that's an awful lot of army ants, and I say they're here for the party. And we sing and dance, sing and laugh, until we're too tired to do anything except cuddle in the pickup under the embroidered quilt from the Ladies' Christian Society back home in Johnston County, North Carolina.

Derek Adams

Pandora and the Flying Dutchman

1940-53

The measure of love is what one is willing to give up for it

Great ropes bind the ship
sadistically to the quayside.
I feel strangely disconnected
life, love, work, lost to me,
exiled to my native land.
The past is not another country
it's the same country it has always been.

Dali & Gala hold court with the press.
Nobody notices a short Jew returning.

Andrew, Yves & Marcel
have settled in New York:
home once, it doesn't fit anymore
like trying to get into
one of my childhood suits
my arms can't bend,
the collar is choking me.

Paris, still occupies my dreams:
the arrogant grey uniforms,
the black spiders that crawl
the walls of the rue de Rivoli.

The long flat road sizzles,
flashes quicksilver in the distance.
Telegraph poles tick past
the speedo taps eighty.

Los Angeles
sun, palms, low houses,
a scent of Spain blows from the south.
If I close my eyes
I could be in Antibes.

Juliet
she holds me in her palm
she opens my eyes
like the lid of an old box
she is blood warming an ancient spirit
she is a candle flame
viewed through red wine.

On this strip of land trapped
between desert and beach,
art is a rare bloom, stunning
as the bright flowers on the cactus,
no one cares
it's left to wither and die.

A commission to paint a portrait,
a Technicolor movie prop,
Ava Gardner as Pandora
holding a box.
Driving through MGM's gates
passing cowboys, gangsters,
sketching Ava between scenes.
At home Juliet stands in
holding a box.

The moon is full, high over the sea,
erotic and disturbing.
I hear the gypsy singer in the tavern below.

The Santa Anna sings like a siren.
The Ocean calls, Paris tugs once more,
will you give up this life for me.

A sea of hands wave from the quayside
the klaxon wails,
smoke weeps from the funnels,
Juliet lights a cigarette.
We stand at the handrail watching
the Lady Liberty, the sky scrapers
sink into the horizon,
the gulls drift away.

Susan Gilmore

Ava in Ottawa

I had to skate clear to Canada
to meet you.
At fourteen, I traced
a dropped, stalled river,
paced the canal
that banks everything on winter,
blades thinning ice into long white smiles.
Back on my family's black-and-white set,
Show Boat sailed, already in progress.
Soapstone warriors mouthed "oh no" from the mantle
as the film rolled through snow and static,
stoic, dubbed.
Watch the Mississippi swell,
hear a man murmur make-believe
to curls, a girl's knees.
French whispered off the tip of his
two-faced tongue,
till homesick American song
took him South:
"Only...I love you...
Only...only...you love me."
I waited—
what could wrap this up but music?—
waited, while chords docked a gray matinee,
till the camera cut you in,
thawed the small screen between us.
Brave Ava,
your delicious tears
spill kisses,
pour over passing wheels,
churn real blood and steam
from cool.

Let the boat go.
Your color trumps.
The voice they took still tells.
Crazy, maybe
I wanted, want
to stay on shore with Ava.
Can't help,
can't help
lovin' till I die.

Barbara Hamby

Working at Pam-Pam's

Ava, darling, skin white as mayonnaise, eyes of cat-scratch topaz,
    zirconia smile, making *Mogambo* with Gable in Africa,
Bwana Clark, to you, baby, Grace Kelly tumbling the substitute daddy,
    you rolling in Swamp Sinatra. What did you see in him—dumb,
crooner from Hoboken, a shrimp, and you in a gal's biggest fix,
    x- and y-chromosomes splitting in your deepest beauty, that toxic
ditch of burping and feeding on the horizon. You think you know
    what the years ahead hold—you left with the baby, Sinatra a cad.
Enemies or lovers—who's to say? Does anyone really change? Henry V,
    Vlad the Impaler, Saint Teresa of Avila—some do, but some
feel sucking the blood from a maiden's neck is all they can manage. You
    understand how beauty can take you only so far. Of course, if
God were in his heaven, we all might be film goddesses rather than fat
    timecard-punching factory workers with lacquered beehives, sewing
halter tops for girls whose primary job will always be painting their nails.
    Such a world begs you to believe in the Hindu idea of *maya*, which
is to say everything is illusion, kind of like the movies or theater or
    remember the time you found your boyfriend with your best friend? I
jump at the idea of *maya*, because though I try to be a vegetarian, barbecue
    quick-stops call to me like roadside sirens: Sonny's, Dreamland, D.J.
Kittrell's, Jim and Milt's. Ava, you started out as a bit player: carhop,
    pretty hatcheck girl, ringsider, and then your gorgeous face was stuck
like candy on magazines and marquees all over the world, sometimes too
    opalescent to be human. When you lay dying in London, did you feel
more alive than ever or was it like the story of Vishnu and the holy man
    Narada, who asks the god for the secret of *maya*. Vishnu says to him,
"Narada, dive into that lake," which he does and emerges a princess, slim,
    married to a powerful king. Her life is golden. She has many children,

owns palaces, her children have children, but her father and husband quarrel,
    lash out at each other until all her family lies dead on the battlefield. No
person has known such grief. Her dear ones lie on the funeral pyre as daybreak
    kindles its fire in the east, and she lights the flame, dives in, and comes up
queen no more, but Narada. "This," says Vishnu, "is *maya's* raj,
    jailer extraordinare. For whom do you weep, Narada?" This is the "Q"
really in "Q & A." For whom do we weep? In dreams we are Richard III,
    ink-stained pen pushers, scullery maids, a hunched-over Laurence Olivier
starring as the evil king on stage, Marilyn Monroe on Harry Cohn's couch.
    Here's to the movie queens with their nose jobs, snow jobs, blow jobs.
"The beauty thing was fun," Ava said later in Madrid walking along,
    gabbing with a friend, passing Pam-Pam's, a local burger joint
under the white sky. "But I'd work at Pam-Pam's before I'd take off
    for Hollywood and star in another crappy movie." O Vishnu,
Vishnu, make me dive into that lake every minute of my misbegotten life,
    every time I forget I'm Narada following the black "V"
wild birds make in an autumn sky. Here's to the mosquito, Lord,
    drinking our blood, be we factory worker, star, wife, widow,
X-rated movie actress, saint, burger flipper, barfly, sporadic mechanic,
    clown or crone. Empty me of everything I am—sphinx, minx,
yogi, yeti, yenta, yodeling nun. Forgive me for being so dense, so numb.
    Break my back with the beauty of the world. Throw me in solitary,
zip me into a shroud. Throw a match on the pyre, rend the veil of *maya*,
    annex me as the Nazis annexed Poland, help me pass your pop quiz.

Charles Rossiter

She Asked for a Joke or a Poem

She could be cured
by the time I write a poem
so I send the joke
which is about chemotherapy
and not very funny,
and I tell her
I'll still love her
without hair,
it will be all right,
and to me she is still the Ava Gardner
in *Night of the Iguana*
who lights up all of Richard Burton's
Mexico.

Now I am thinking
of parties long ago,
like the night Jack scribbled
"I love Allen Ginsberg—
let that be recorded
in heaven's unchangeable
heart—"
    and now Jack's dead.

or the night we played pool
and drank beer for hours
after hours of champagne,

the rest gone home,
stood in the driveway
and missed the dawn.
    Ava Gardner, I tell her.

It will be all right.

Virgil Suarez

American Drag Rhapsody:
J. Edgar Hoover in Havana

He always came to the Tropicana Night Club in Old Havana,
a touch of Yves Saint Laurent perfume behind the ears, a contact
would meet him there and then take him to the underground

gay nightclubs, where the free-for-all made his head spin,
after the *mojitos* and all the bump-and-grind action, he'd go
home with the blond who caressed his face with smooth dove-

feather hands, tickled him on the soft backs of his knees, licked
him there where the sultry Cuban men liked to give *la espuela*
a trick they learned from the French, that much he was sure

of—ah, those nights in Havana, those young men who knew him
better than his own mother. Music pulsing behind stucco walls,
a light glinting off a chandelier…these nights of release

from daily tensions. The games he played. His favorite scene
of any movie was Ava Gardner's scene with the two dark and
handsome boys in *Night of the Iguana*, shot in Acapulco.

He liked this bite-squeeze of flesh, no doubt. One night he
painted his lips bright red, put on a flamenco dress, sunset red,
white polka dots the size of quarters on the ruffles, onyx shiny

pumps, and he danced in front of mirrors, some distant guitar
weep and clatter of castanets helped him keep the rhythm. Nobody
knew him at the Havana Hilton, not here, not there at the clubs.

He loved this anonymity, this disappearing act of vanishing
before mirrors. Silk scarves around his neck, cotton blouses
rubbing against his nipples. Oh those glorious Havana

mornings when he opened the windows to let some light sneak in:
people below on the move, the bakery boys coming in to work
the dough with their rough fingers, pigeons on the wires, a man

on a balcony with a cigarette in his mouth, smoke wisping
in the wind. Holy Evanescence. How many mornings like this
would he have left in the world? How many nights would he feel

this rapture of passion, unbridled, free? The young man behind
him embracing him to greet the day like lovers, the way men
have held each other into an eternity.

Gail Wronsky

Cirque du Liz and Dick

Puerto Vallarta

Facing each other rather desperately—
his eye is like a star—
we stare and say, "Well, we have come this far."

She doesn't like the lizards, strewn
like dry white bones
all over everything.

Nor the way stiletto heels sink
in the soft Moroccan tile that is
ubiquitous.

He drinks, and looks so bloody handsome.
Who dya think he'll make love to, Mrs. Burton—
Sue Lyons or Ava Gardner?

She feels discarded, fooling with her pearls
in the reptile torpor of the Mexican
Riviera. Key grips always

booming away somewhere beyond the patio.
He wants to be with her in London,
eating Lemon pies. He longs for

the old delightful tracking down of
gloves to match a blouse or
just her drag queen whimsy.

Here it's all *La Vida no vale nada.*
Life is worth nothing.
Part of her is sorry she became

a public utility.
Part of him wants to do Hamlet again.
But he feels closer to Claudius,

Marrying so quickly on top of the death
of the other marriage. A woman
is like glass, they say here:

always in danger.
Together,
they've renamed the town Seething—

They still have that feeling of antenna—
a quivering contact with each other.
"Above her head she poses

another spray of artificial roses,"
making him think of a novelty rodeo act
he saw a very long time ago in Wales.

Joseph Donahue

With Lulu at the Beach
for Stephen-Paul Martin

A headlong pitch
shattering the whisky rack.
A pistol in Jackie O's hand...
Dallas did not happen. The
motorcade & magic bullet were a lie.
(Kennedy died in a liquor store in New York City.)
Festival of blood & broken bottles & a last gasp: *Find Bobby!*
The white flame shoots up: & inside the blaze
the driver moves untroubled & slow
& the cab turns to ash
& his wife watches tape
& his daughter on the phone
Knight of Infinite Resignation
bedridden & devious &
dying untransgressed by the lithium...
Or: naked before a face taped on a mirror
ecstatic & trembling: jagged hair checked by a flower
as stunning as her words are sad:
their crumpled pavilion
a green silk pallor freshened by an interior gasp –
Or: one thought, over & over. Or mania's desolate glimmer as
threadless through a shattered maze O
Irish rat berhymned...
Riot room, a whiff of tear gas.
The time has come. Turn off the tape
& talk candidly with the Strangler
& only one of many survives the plunge
& he remembers nothing of the plane
& nurses or flight attendants
at the airport medical tent murmur

they're often like that at first…
& our biographies are
a scattering of ocean soaked clothes
& mourners drift wailing from one heap to the next.
The comedian flayed, new music pours from the mouth of a horse.
A whacked dithyramb. Awaited eons, in darkness.
Erzule, goddess and film maker, would lead you
through the cool shadowy leaves
a jungle apocastasis
but you wander off the path
& into wild bursts of heat and light…
& when the surge falls back
angelic cages & hotel parrots
fresh juice, mood pills, & in the distance
the blue puff of plastic-wrapped banana trees…
Alright, alright. This time you
be the Consul, & I'll be Yvonne…
Night. Doleful drumming. Negligee & veil.
Demons swirling in the marriage cup
soul cut free of the body
& other crude cinematic tricks.
Pilfered crypt, zombie backdrop –
A man in blackface points out
the interior & the sugar harvest
uninterrupted by night. The high breaks.
Nothing helps. Daylong rainy dark.
Deposed in the blue sphere of
my circumnavigations
& Traherne hymns seraphic
in his era of sweetness & terror…
Earth & air, fire & water
A cyclical & ill desire…
World well broken. Shack on a reef.
Nothing's left of that first astonishment
but the candid notations of a great man's navigator.
Step from the boats, gods of caste, tenancy, bacterial rapture…
Beneath all the upheaval it was an image of herself
within herself & hidden from herself…

And what origin will achieve the
ravishment of witness...
& then you flare all
sexiness & wit, a dazzle
in this palace of lobby art
& desktop calendars...
A day with Lulu at the beach...
But you should know, you say,
I am also elsewhere, now, & drowning
sending dreams to you across what distance...
On TV: a man with cameras
implanted in his eyes. He blinks.
A screen goes blank. He takes yellow pills.
He never sleeps. He must convince
a dying woman to allow
a film crew at her deathbed...
& the sun ripped from the poster
& all goes spray paint,
our drained embrace
in fluorescent zombie light
our kisses a wrecked cassette tape
shimmering in the trees, & burning oleanders.
Toxic Florida. Smoke over green muck.
What missionary infection marred our holiday...
& how many weapons named after people can you name?
Colt Bowie. Guillotine? Not really a weapon. Lance,
after Launcelot. Crossbow, after Clara Bow.
Gatling, Derringer, Stamp, Big Bertha, & so
of each moment, its utopian tatter...
I won't drop hints but I won't look away.
My words are harmless, you can forget them.
But later you'll be burning, reckless with intimation...
A pure beginning? What god can conjure it?
Or let mind rejoice in its mysteries
as cell by cell intention builds a body, as arc
to a blinding scroll, at the hour the rabbi unseals it
& lifts the translation of a world. He moves among the remnant
lofting delicately that which without ritual

would be a defilement to look upon
& all desire themselves unraveled and read
& gathered into an intelligence, or so I thought
in warm rain at the locked gate, that
first temple in the New World…
Or let rivers unblock, or let green
land rise or torment beat you untillered
& towards no home as angels in gold fire
dispose of messages…

The Reverend Shannon
has retired from Blake's Tours.
He sits with Ava Gardner
overlooking the sea. The
lesbian Baptist voice teacher
from hell has left. The Mexicans
are bare-chested, & dance in the cabana.
He no longer feels the need to kneel
beside sleeping ingénue outcasts.
The Protestant muse has left
some poppy seed tea. Of the cross
& the tourbus distributor cap,
those emblems of divine
& earthly power,
he has, through what,
with some irony, was called
a voluptuous crucifixion,
divested himself…

Kirpal Singh

Enchanted Dreams & Lost Hopes:
Amarjit's Whisky Goes Awry

"YOU KNOW, the best thing about Ava Gardner, my gawd, you should see her inner thigh—simply creamy, just inviting, waiting for your caress—"

"How would you know? You talk as if you had her-"

"But I did yaar, I did."

"Yiah—I am sure—in your dreams."

"Yes."

It is now more than seven years since that dialogue took place. We were all a little pissed, on Fifth Avenue New York, hearing the wails of sirens and the catcalls of those who thought we were truly aliens. There were four of us—Amarjit, a newly graduated engineer from Purdue University come to the east to seek a better fortune; Sarjit, the lawyer whose job was mainly to frame everything for his colleagues in Smith & Smith but not appear in court himself; Harvinder, Amarjit's brother, who had come from Malaysia to entice his brother to return home because their parents were getting old and missing their firstborn; and me, yes, me—I had newly arrived in New York from Singapore to be interviewed for a possible appointment at Columbia—one of the great universities of the world where I was hoping to become an agent of real change so the university could truly usher in the new millennium with flourish. And, oh yes, I must not forget Jenny—Jenny was Sarjit's white American girlfriend. Jenny was a painter, an artist whose own parents had written her off.

Poor Amarjit. He really loved the US of A. His parents had spent tens of thousands to get him educated at what everyone considered one of the best engineering schools in the world. And he had done very well, scoring top grades in every examination. Upon graduation he got a job immediately, in a small firm in Indiana. But he was unhappy because, as he told us, there really was no future in the small firm, and he had been advised to go east for better prospects. So, now in New York, Amarjit was drinking his life away, refusing to return home to Malaysia or to acknowledge, like Sarjit, that life for aliens like him was going to be tough. The blacks—or Afro-Americans as they were increasingly being labeled—didn't welcome the likes of Amarjit for reasons which still remain unfathomable in spite of numerous theories of competition being put forward by various sociologists; the Hispanics, who were a growing number, just didn't want anyone whose command of English was better (and almost everyone's was!); and the whites, aaahh, yes, the whites, they always said the best of things but did little to actually help Amarjit get a good job! Jenny's explanation for this was "We whites have a super love-hate thing for you guys; we actually admire you for your hard work, commitment, and dedication, but are not sure if you are going to make us brown by marrying our girls." Then she would laugh, ironically, sardonically, sadly. I knew that her relationship with Sarjit was a real contributing factor to her parents' indifference to what she was so desperately trying to achieve as an artist.

"You know what though," said Amarjit, more thoughtfully, "she was simply adorable in *On the Beach*. Any of you see that beautiful film? Based on the novel by Nevil Shute? Hey, you (pointing at me), surely you must have seen it, after all, aren't you into books and all that?"

Yes. I was into books except that for my immediate purpose I was not into the kind of books that Columbia, for all its talk of openness, was really keen on. But yes, I had read Shute's novel and seen the film. It was science fiction to me.

And very Australian. And, yes, I remembered Ava Gardner's role—stunning, not quite vampish, but highly sexual. But we were in America, and Ava Gardner had died a sad, lingering death and, never, I thought, found lasting joy in any of her marriages or relationships. For me it was *The Night of the Iguana* which was her best film. I remembered watching that as quite a young boy but never forgot the tied iguana. Later as I grew up I realized that the iguana was such an apt symbol for so many of us—yearning to be free but trapped in our own prisons. Even here, in New York, I could see how apt the symbolism was. Amarjit was in a prison.

"Yes, of course, Amarjit, but I still prefer the novel. I think Ava Gardner should have suicided like the character in Shute's novel which she portrays. Would have made it a much better film."

"Maybe," said Amarjit, "but you know Ava Gardner. She was not made for death, my *dhost*; she was made for life. For giving life vitality, especially the vitality of sex which keeps us all alive."

"Speak for yourself," said Sarjit.

"Is there nothing you guys talk about but sex?" intervened Jenny. "You know we white girls may be attracted to you guys, but we are not dumb. And we are not your sex slaves."

"Of course not, honey," said a meek Sarjit.

I felt for Jenny. I almost knew by instinct she was finding the four of us Sikhs a little tiresome; our sense of humour was not exactly hers, though because of her love for Sarjit (Amarjit, though, was convinced it was not love but pity), she tolerated our ranting and raving and carrying on. Fifth Avenue New York was enchanting—I had heard so much about it that being there now, physically, was for me almost out-of-this-world. I saw drunks lying around; I saw couples hugging and kissing; I saw executives hurrying and hurrying; I saw old people being told to get out of the way by indifferent young people; I saw wonderful stores selling expensive, branded clothing and goods; I saw some superlative cars making their presences felt as the traffic crawled; I saw people, with aimlessness in their eyes, strolling, staring, stopping, window-shopping. Was this, seriously, the place I wanted to be if Columbia did offer me a job? My reverie was interrupted—or, rather, I was supposed to be part of Amarjit's rave.

"You see, even you have come here from your blighted Singapore to seek greener pastures. This is what America is all about. Living your dream. This is the land of the brave and free, people, brave and free. Hey, you again, you man of books, what is that book, that book about the American dream, etc? You know the one I mean by Fitzgerald…"

"I think you mean *The Great Gatsby*…"

"That's the one. Correct. Ava Gardner would have made a brilliant Daisy—the woman whose allure is simply irresistible. The woman all men fall for. Oh man, if only I could have one Ava Gardner in my life. You, Sarjit, are a bloody lucky bugger man—you have Jenny."

This was a little too close to the bone. Among Sikh men it was not proper to refer to a friend's partner, even in jest. In fact, especially in jest.

"Are you flattering me?" asked Jenny, whose eyes lit up as he queried Amarjit?

"No, my dear, I am telling Sarjit what a lucky bastard he is having got you. He should forget about what they call him and just marry you. After all a towel-head who wins the hand of a beautiful white girl can't be that bad!"

Amarjit had crossed the line. He has spoken the unspeakable. Racism was not a subject any of us were comfortable about. I had been warned about discrimination by my colleagues, but my answer to them had been it exists everywhere. The difference was in degree.

Sarjit was not going to let this go. Amarjit's remarks were not only hurtful but an affront. Sarjit had been suffering snobbery ever since he made up his mind to live in New York and work at Smith & Smith. Jenny was his consolation. In her and in her paintings he found the much-needed transcendence he, as a lawyer, did not always find in the law books. But Amarjit's utterance had made the inner truth, the outer stigma, come alive.

I remember Sarjit hitting Amarjit hard on the head and Amarjit stumbling. Jenny was shocked and clasped Harvinder tight. For his part Harvinder was speechless for he was not succeeding in persuading Amarjit to return. I, well, I, the man of books, I pushed Sarjit to one side of the pavement and held him there. It was obvious to me that Fifth Avenue New York was not going to sympathize with our sorry state except to savor the fact that we aliens were yet another source for their merriment; for with the corner of my eye I saw a group of boys laughing at what they had just witnessed.

"Okay, okay, I'm sorry," said Amarjit. "It's the fucking beer you fed me just now."

"*Teri mah dhi*," said Sarjit.

"What did Sarjit just say?" asked Jenny

"Nothing. Don't worry."

Throughout the shenanigans I tried to maintain my cool. I was an obvious outsider, except, perhaps, for Harvinder who clearly was even more determined that the time had truly come for his brother to return to Malaysia and be with the family.

We walked on after the incident. Surely the night was not going to end this way, with a fight and ensuing sullenness. I decided to speak up.

"Hey, Amarjit, you know all that you said about Ava Gardner? Well I think we have our very own Ava Gardners. Many of them vying for the same titles, trying their luck in the same film yards, craving the same glories. But ours dare not take the risks. And for me the real Ava Gardner is that near-tragic woman who took risks, with everything. Like Jenny here who has risked a lot to pursue her passion for art. Maybe this is where we should all stop and reconsider our lives. Do we want to stay safe or take risks?"

There was a faint smile playing on their lips. There was a look of expectancy in Jenny's eyes as she still held close to Harvinder who was beginning to feel a little uneasy. Sarjit managed to put his embarrassment behind him and say, "America is not for the weak – and also not for those who just think scoring high grades in exams is the answer to making millions. America is for those who are in for the long haul. America is for those of us who believe in a dream and are prepared to suffer for it."

We all seem to have sobered up. Now there was this other dialogue starting. About America. About the great US of A. About us who were brought up on Hollywood movies. Jenny, Sarjit, Harvinder, and I looked at Amarjit who had been silent.

"Alright, Harvinder. I think mah and pah are right. You are right. America is not for me. I should return to Malaysia. The *bunga raya* still smells good. My days of whisky and rye are over. The beer here is cheap, but the dreams are expensive. Let us go."

Well, what could we say or do after these odd remarks from Amarjit except slowly move away from each other after wishing good-nights. Jenny held Sarjit's hand, but I knew the clasp had been weakened. Harvinder put his arms around Amarjit as he slowly steered towards a taxi.

And I, well, I thought about my Columbia interview and slowly trudged towards my hotel thinking "If Columbia offers me a job, that will be my risk."

All this took place seven years ago. How time truly passes.

Cathryn Essinger

On the Beach

As a liberal-arts major all of my life,
I take great comfort in knowing
that the astronauts are out there,
patching the Hubble telescope
with 100-mph duct tape and string.

For that matter, I want to meet
the man who first slid a human heart
into a Playmate Cooler and stepped
onto a commercial flight. Did he confess
to the attendant or did she assume
bologna and cheese and a six pack?

Is it really such a leap from archaeology
to leftovers? If Tupperware can preserve
last week's pickled beets, why not
a prehistoric brain? Resourcefulness
is overrated…Why, even I might have
thought of Superglue, when Freddie
the Pelican flew home with a broken bill.

And if Max the gorilla at the Toledo zoo
is having trouble reproducing his kind,
a little porno flick from the Congo
might do him good. If his mate,
hand raised in Philadelphia,
has become so civilized that she doesn't
know which end is up, put the baby
in Pampers and give her a break.
Everyone has shortcomings.

Even math majors forget
to balance checkbooks and who knows
if the scientists are right?
Despite their smug superiority,
is anyone really going to question
data gathered from the outer
reaches of the solar system?

It's easy to be critical I suppose
when one has chosen a safe profession.
I've never neglected to thaw out
someone's embryo, or mistyped blood,
or accused someone of a crime
because I misread the DNA scan.
No lives hang in the balance
if I misquote Yeats or forget
who wrote *The Ring and the Book*.

But at the end, when the software
fails and the radiation is rising,
I think that even an English major
will be resourceful enough to loop
the string of the window sash to the neck
of the Coke bottle, balanced
to tap out some erratic Morse Code
to a world half annihilated
by the wonders of modern science.

Ian Rosales Casocot

Old Movies

ON GOOD DAYS, Mother comes out of her room in an Ava Gardner stupor. She is a sinewy siren with mischief in her hair. She has a glass of Scotch in her hand, daintily handled. She lights a cigarette, and blows smoke into my face, all the while keeping an ice maiden stance perfected after so many nights watching Kim Novak in *Vertigo*. Auntie Nida, on the way to the kitchen, pinches her ass while I gag from the smoke. "Stop that, Charo," Auntie Nida tells her, "the boy's only ten."

"The boy's a bastard," Mother quickly says. Then she laughs, the ashes from her cigarette spilling into the slinky black of her Holly Golightly dress. She ruffles my 10-year old hair and coos. "Don't you just look like your father, Jaggy? Named after him, too. Travis the bastard. All Travises are bastards, yes?"

"Charo! You're drunk," Auntie Nida hisses from far away, cloistered with her chopping boards and black-bottomed skillets. There are telltale odors of *escabeche* stealing into the room.

Sometimes, I catch a flicker of life in Mother's tipsy eyes. "Ma?" I ask.

"Ava," she will insist, her voice a bit more throaty.

It never usually lasts long. Ava Gardner fades away, always by the second glass of Scotch.

"Come on, Jaggy," she will then say. "I suppose we can watch a movie in my room now."

I do not remember much what sobriety can be. On bad days when she is not Ava Gardner, or Kim Novak, or Lolita Rodriguez, Mother is a weeping shadow, her room locked and curtained off—her darkness as dramatic as the lull before an evening's last full show.

People call me Jaguar, like the wild animal, for no apparent reason except that under proper lighting, I can pass of as a young Philip Salvador. My name is Travis actually, because that was how my Auntie Nida remembered my father's name when I was born. This I learn later on.

My father's name was Travis, and he was a security guard over at the big pawnshop on San Juan Street. He had a motorcycle and a killer mustache, and told everybody he was once a taxidriver from Carcar, Cebu. Other than that, there was nothing else to remember about him except his face in a terrified blur—people said—as he cranked his way out of town on his motorcycle the day after my mother's water broke during dinner at Lolong's house, and fainted dead away.

That was the first time everyone knew she was pregnant—and laboring. "But she was so small, her tummy was so small—she was wearing baggy clothes all the time. Nobody knew!" Auntie Nida would now say, if anybody at all cared to ask. Pregnancies were a dime a dozen.

Everyone thought mother just peed over the bad *escabeche*.

She had been sick the past few months, Auntie Nida remembered. Refused to eat anything, except hamburgers, which she ate constantly. She had grown pale and was dizzy most days—would not see the doctor even, despite Auntie Nida's constant nagging.

"I'm fine. I'm fine," Mother would say.

Nay Gloria, Mother's cousin, swore to Auntie Nida that mother was getting out of bed at the strangest hours of the night, to vomit at the upstairs toilet. Nay Gloria would ask, "Are you all right?"—rubbing her eyes to squint into the garish whiteness of the fluorescent tiles.

"I'm fine. I'm fine," Mother would say.

Food poisoning. And they would go back to bed, and Nay Gloria would think, yes, the fish was bad that evening at supper, and perhaps Nanang Conching could get fresher meat next time? Nanang Conching was getting careless. It was very difficult to get good help these days.

So nobody saw it coming. Not that night, when Lolong was telling everybody at the dinner table that the mayor of the town was up to some dirty tricks. "How the fool got elected is beyond me," he boomed, just as Nanang Conching was serving the food.

Auntie Nida was nagging along, too: "Perhaps you can eat proper, Charo, Inday. None of those hamburgers now. Bad for you. Bad meat—I hear they use cats for meat, those restaurants. Catburgers! Ay, the horror. Here, Nanang made some fish *escabeche*." She scooped a piece into mother's plate, and ladled a generous amount of the sweet brown sauce over it. Then Mother's water broke, and she fainted at the shock.

Lolong thundered. "What in God's name ...?"

Nobody was able to eat the *escabeche* except Pudding the cat, but by that time everyone was in the car. Four in the back—mother, Auntie Nida, Nay Gloria, Lolita the neighbor—and three in the front—Dodong the driver, Lolong, and Gerardo, Lolita's son—, which made the whole car quite tight, but nobody seemed to notice or to care, except mother who was beginning to come around, and was screaming.

"Breathe now, Charo, like a good girl—huff, huff, huff—you wretched child! How can you be so stupid! Why didn't you tell anyone you were pregnant, for God's sake! Breathe!"

Mother went on screaming.

Lolong fumed. "It's that Travis ba, inday? Putsa! Oh Jesus. Are you all right, inday? Are you? This is crazy. Where's the hosp—?" Mother's screams drowned out Lolong's voice.

"Now, now, just breathe, okay?" Auntie Nida said. She was holding her arm over mother's head, and wiping mother's sweat from her brow with a tissue paper. "Are we there yet, Dong? Can't you hurry, you turtle, you son of a bitch? Have you been drinking again?"

"No, ma'am," slurred Dodong the driver, as mother screamed some more.

In the grim rush, everything seemed like an old Buster Keaton sketch—slapstick tragedy, with no screen irises to fade off the scene, only breathing and cramped space to puncture the soundtrack of tires screeching, and mother screaming.

"Breathe now, Charo, breathe," Auntie Nida said.

"I can't breathe!" Mother screamed. "I can't breathe!"

"Well then, maybe you should have thought of that before you got yourself knocked up," Auntie Nida said angrily, and then in a beat: "Is Travis really the father?"

Mother screamed.

Nobody saw the car that came from the right of an intersection, rammed into them, and turned like tootsie roll melting on a hot day. Their car skidded to the sidewalk, and crashed, wrapping itself around an electric pole. But they were packed in so tight they just bounced a little bit—except for Dodong the driver who flew through the windshield like a paper plane and landed a good ten meters away with head cracked open like a ripe watermelon.

When the police and the ambulance arrived, which was a long time, I burst through with a wail, into the backseat. Nay Gloria would later tell me there was blood and glass everywhere. Mother had fainted again, and Auntie Nida was screaming. Lolong just kept muttering, "Travis... Sorry. Sorry..." before senile dementia took over, almost on the spot, and he was seen walking around the car, talking to his friend Mike, who had already been dead twelve years. Lolong was 62.

Auntie Nida named me Travis, "to make us all remember this *lecheng yawa*, this night," but she couldn't really think of anything by the time the ambulance screeched into the hospital, and the nurse was pestering her for the father's family name. "Travis...Travis..." she just said.

"That would be the father's name, ma'am. And his last name?"

"*Peste*, I don't know his last name!"

"Okay, then. I take it the mother's...single?"

Auntie Nida wheeled around like a mad bull. "The child's a bastard, okay? Call him Travis, if you want, just like that bastard." And like a willowy Delia Razon, she crumpled to the floor weeping and shaking.

"Is this story true?" I prod Nay Gloria when I'm old enough to listen, and ask. "It's a little too dramatic."

"*Ambot, 'noy, uy,*" she shrugs. "If you don't ask questions, you don't get lies—or worse, the truth." Nay Gloria sighs. "Then again, I could be lying. I don't know ... Go ask your mother."

But Mother is too busy being Bette Davis.

My name is Travis Silayan. I have my mother's eyes. I don't look like my father. I should know: I have seen him tucked away in my mother's purse when she is in bed, endlessly and silently watching old movies on her TV, as if she is waiting for nothing to come from the cold of the night, and only has this vicarious comfort of the dark and the flickering pictures before her.

Cofradia. Casablanca. Gone With the Wind. Shane. The Betamax whirs away the silent nights.

The whirring is my first memory.

Sometimes she settles for something new, but the new ones are almost always violent and terrifying—"This is the romance of the present," she murmurs to me when she re-members I am watching the movie with her.

We do not sit near each other.

"I named you after Robert DeNiro in *Taxi Driver,* you know," she says. "You had killer eyes, like Travis Bickle."

I am five. I do not know who Robert DeNiro is.

Later she tells me she doesn't really know why my name is Travis. "Your Auntie Nida named you Travis. Go ask her," she whispers, and turns away.

I have no memory of my mother not crying.

The man in the photo has chinky eyes and short hair gelled back. He slings a black coat over his shoulders, "like James

Dean," mother tells me. She does not care I am rifling through her things.

He poses with peacock masculinity astride his motorcycle—of a vintage model that I once have seen in one of those magazines. But it is an old photo. The colors are almost gone, and the borders are frayed with time. And the spot where his face is is somehow faded, but you can still see the tentative smile, and the way it crinkles his eyes.

I am six when I first see the picture, and I think the man strange. Nobody I know poses like that, not even Lino the doctor who comes now and then to check on Lolong and my increasingly frail mother. Not Noy Ishmael—Ishmá, Nanang Conching's husband—who has become our driver after Dodong. (Nobody is allowed to talk about the past.)

Certainly not Lolong who is doubled up most days in geriatric gravity, and snaps without his dentures at everybody, and demands to see Lolang night after night.

"But Nanay's gone, 'Tay. You should know that," Auntie Nida tells him, as she leads him to bed.

"What do you mean, woman?" Lolong booms back. "She was just here a moment ago, showing me this beautiful child…this beautiful child…"

"Okay, 'Tay."

"Do you know that beautiful child's name?"

"No, I don't, 'Tay."

"Aw, you wouldn't know, anyhow. It was Charo. Yes. Sweet Charo. She was a beautiful child."

"Okay, 'Tay."

"What are we talking about? Who are you, woman?"

"It's Nida, 'Tay. Your eldest daughter."

"I don't have a daughter," he snaps. "I'm not even married yet."

Auntie Nida looks old for her age.

"You are so Rock Hudson," Steve tells me. We are sitting up in bed past midnight, watching TNT. Marlon Brando is screaming "Stella!" and rips his shirt. Stella comes down the stairs, swaying in the wanton heat.

"And I suppose you want to be my Doris Day?" I tell him, as I catch my breath. In the darkness I reach for his hand. He gives me a squeeze. I tell him I love the way the bluish tint of the TV bounces off his curly hair.

Steve laughs, and turns serious. "Come on, Travis. This is the '90s, you know. You really don't have to hide who you are anymore, not from your family. Did you know that they published *Ladlad* last year, and it has since been flying off the shelves? I don't know what that tells you—"

I sigh. "It tells me nothing."

Steve reaches for the remote control and turns the TV mute. "Something. It tells you to be open is to be free."

I grin. "You talk like a goddam queenie activist."

"Jesus, Jag, we're too old for these things."

"I am only 26."

"Well, I am telling you the truth. And you know why Jason Gould's gay."

"Who's Jason Gould?"

"Barbra Streisand's son."

We laugh. "I think I know what you're talking about," I tell Steve. "Still, my mother's my mother."

"It's always someone's mother," Steve says.

In my constant nightmares, Mother becomes a crazed Joane Crawford, immortalized by Faye Dunaway as *Mommie Dearest*, shouting "No more wirehangers!" I picture her with a glass of Scotch in her hand, spilling liquor down my face.

"Jag," Steve says after a while, "do you remember Humphrey Bogart in *The Maltese Falcon*? Do you remember he was cold and hard, like his name, Sam Spade? He beats up Joel Cairo—the Peter Lorre character—not just because he has to, but because Cairo carries a perfumed handkerchief. Get it? You know what that meant in a 1941 movie."

Maybe we watch too many movies. Just too many Judy Garland musicals.

I am eight when I manage to read the note at the back of the photograph: "To Charo. *Sa atong kaugmaon*, Travis"—and think how strange it is for this man to also have my name. But stranger things have been said to me. That I am a "special" child, for one thing.

"Like Jesus, you know?" Nay Gloria says. "Only not holy." She is flustered. "Oh, you know what I mean..."

"No, I don't," I tell her.

I am exasperated with the evasiveness of adults. My Grade Two teacher, for example, tells me I am too far advanced from my other classmates. I have an urge to tell her that is what you get when you have watched Judy Holliday ten thousand times in *Born Yesterday* since you were five.

Nay Gloria sighs. She is still unmarried. She lives with a friend named Carmen.

"Okay, Jaguar," Nay Gloria is saying. "This is what I mean. You ask me who your father is? Nobody knows. Maybe your birth was some kind of...of an, uh, Immaculate Conception, just like Mama Mary. You know?"

I'm eight. I don't exactly know what she means. But it sounds nice. Chocolate Connection. Which is like the name of the ice cream Nay Gloria buys me when we go to the movies with Tita Carmen. They are always happy, and are always glad to take me along with them, "as long as you remain quiet and be a good big boy that you already are." I nod gratefully, because I like real movies—the big ones on screen, and because my mother never takes me anywhere anymore.

Nay Gloria and Tita Carmen buy me popcorn and Pepsi, and if I want, they will buy me ice cream, too. I stuff myself as *E.T.* flickers in the dark. There is something about Elliott that makes me understand. And he has the most beautiful eyes on a boy I have ever seen.

Lolong mistakes me for a mirror while I am dressing to go out with Gerardo and the gang. He has been too cranky lately—78 years old and making everyone miserable. Only mother seems content with his old age.

I wonder when the old coot will die.

Lolong studies my face. "Oh my God...Oh my God," he whispers, almost afraid.

"Lolong, are you okay?" I steady his shaking hands. The

faint brown blotches on his skin snake like a curse. His skin feels cold and balmy. For a moment, clarity enters his eyes, and he regards me with the careful scrutiny of an interested, yet wary, stranger.

"Charo?" he croaks.

"Mother is in her room, Lolong," I tell him. "She's tired. She's watching a Shirley Temple movie." She is not. She is crying again, and refuses to see me.

I tell all these to Gerardo when he comes up the drive in his new red Jeep.

"Forgive the old man, Jaguar," Gerardo says, as we drive to the Dumaguete Music Box. "I remember, when you were born and we had that accident—I think I was six—he went completely nuts. Never recovered from it. I suppose he remembers you during that time."

"I was a baby. Nobody remembers a baby's face."

"I remember you. When you plopped out into the backseat, you did not cry. You boomed."

I fidget with the car radio. Soon I clear the air with Madonna singing "Papa Don't Preach." We have our high school girls to score with. I am 18, a virgin. I am ready. I am enthusiastic. I am eager for the bravado of beer.

Tonight, Mother dies of ovarian cancer. I suppose she must die from something. She has already been dead a long time.

She does not tell anybody she has the disease until she emerges one day from her room, her face a frightened blur, clutching her groin in a staggered fashion to Auntie Nida's room, screaming from the pain, and fainting dead away.

That was the first time everyone knew she was sick—and dying.

Everyone thought mother would just fade away, like the iris vanishing point of her old movies. Nobody sees her around anymore.

She did not tell anyone she was cringing, night after day, from the pain, from deep inside her, for the past months. Auntie Nida only knew she had refused to eat anything, even hamburgers. She had grown pale and was dizzy most days—would not see the doctor even, despite Nay Gloria's constant nagging.

"I'm fine. I'm fine," mother would say.

Tita Carmen swore to Nay Gloria that mother was getting out of bed at the strangest hours of the night, to cry at the upstairs toilet. "Are you all right?" Tita Carmen would ask her, partly irritated from the constant visits, which interrupted her sleep and Nay Gloria's, their bedroom only a jump away from the creaky toilet door.

"I'm fine. I'm fine," my mother said. "Just remembering Tatay, that's all."

Lolong has been dead six months.

And they went back to bed, and Tita Carmen thought that perhaps she could oil the hinges of the toilet doors tomorrow. The house was getting old, and its occupants even older, and crankier. It was very difficult to get good sleep these days.

So nobody saw it coming. Not until that night when mother screamed.

I remember that night. I am in Steven's arms. We have finished watching *Spartacus*. We try to memorize Laurence Olivier's poolside seduction of Tony Curtis. We are hungry for oysters and snails.

Now we are watching Ingmar Bergman's *The Seventh Seal* at Lolong's house when the call comes from the hospital. "It's Auntie Charo," Nay Gloria cries on the phone. It takes forever for her to speak intelligibly. She breathes deeply. "Jaggy, your mother's dead."

"I suppose," I finally say.

Something collapses inside me, but, as yet, there are no tears. Mother, I think, has cried for me all these years. The coincidence of moments is suddenly too strange: death coming in as I am seeing Death—hooded and ominous, cinematic—playing chess with the knight. A negotiation.

It is easier to think of yesterday when—

When I visit her in the hospital, and she sits up in bed, eating an apple, and smiling. I have never really seen my mother smile.

"Hi."

"Hello, Ma," I hesitate.

She laughs weakly and puts the half-finished apple away. She looks terrible and cheap—Loni Anderson after the facelift. "How very *An Affair to Remember*. Do you remember how that scene with Deborah Kerr goes after she sees Cary Grant again after the accident, and he comes up to her and says a nonchalant hello?"

"Yes, Ma."

"Deborah Kerr goes, 'And all I could ever say back was hello'... That was a sad movie, wasn't it? It was the sadness that made it more beautiful, I think."

"Yes, Ma."

"Is your mother still beautiful?"

"Yes, Ma. You look like Ali McGraw."

"Ah, *Love Story*. Do you remember that? Ali McGraw dying of a dreadful disease, yet growing more beautiful by the minute. Hollywood's beautiful, Jaggy. I just wish life could be a little bit more like that."

"I'm sorry, Ma."

"I'm sorry, Travis."

This is the longest conversation we've ever had.

"Ma, I'm—."

She looks at me quietly, and nods faintly. "I can understand," she gently says. She closes her eyes, and I move to the door. Her voice, weak now, stops me.

"Travis never touched me, you know," I hear her say. "But he promised to take me away—away from all that fright. But I guess he forgot. I guess he got too frightened. Your Lolong was capable of anything, even when he was already getting old."

"I know."

"I'm sorry, *hijo*, I could have been more of a mother, you know? Like Ann Revere—"

"*National Velvet*. Elizabeth Taylor was just 12."

"—or somebody. Like one of those Brady Bunch."

"Mr. Brady died of AIDS."

"Yes, but all we really remember are the toothpaste

smiles."

"The toothpaste smiles…"

"I still can be Mrs. Brady, you know."

"I suppose."

"Just give me time, okay?"

I nod.

There is silence, punctuated only by the soothing whir of the air-conditioning. I move to the television to turn it on, and to the light switches to turn them off. This is the only right scenario: the silence, the blue hue of the muted TV screen, and the encompassing darkness.

"Goodnight, ma."

But I think I have always known this is coming. Now, I push down the cradle of the telephone with my fingers, and Nay Gloria becomes a persistent buzz in my ears. I have promised my mother I will not cry: I can only see around me and breathe in the comforting darkness, and hear the soundtrack the scene will have wrought—John Williams as he takes me to the stars? Nino Rota, perhaps, with a haunting score, as beautifully sad as the trembling of my feet. I slowly walk now to where Steve lies sleeping, waiting for my arms to engulf him goodnight. He wakes a little, buzzes my cheek, and whispers: "Is it all over?"

"Yes." I, too, speak softly.

"I'm sorry."

"I know."

"We'll see her tomorrow, Jag."

"I know."

"Okay, then, good night."

"Okay."

In the dark of the room, the blue shadows still flicker, but they only lull me to sleep. The last thing I remember is the solicitous dusk, which is the authority of dreams, the keeper to the vicarious life that becomes the seeking hearts' devoted companion. Steve, Lolong, Auntie Nida, Mother, my so-called father, my so-called life—and this, my redemption, my wishes for a happy ending: they all collide in a dreamy sepia kaleidoscope, and I breathe deeply. Like the old films, the night fades, and I descend into the movies of my dreams.

Robert Rodriguez

from Planet Terror

The Rapist	(muffled) You like Ava Gardner?
Cherry Darling	Sorry?
The Rapist	(takes off gas mask) Ava Gardner. D' you like her?
Cherry	Yeah, I guess.
The Rapist	I was just thinkin' that you, uh, kinda look like Ava Gardner, a little bit. (stops elevator and turns back to Cherry) You have somethin' you wanna say to me?
Cherry	I have nothing to say to you.
The Rapist	You have nothing to say to me? That's funny, cuz I could've sworn you just gave me a "fuck you" look right now. You wanna say "fuck you" to me?
Cherry	Not at this moment.
The Rapist	(pulls gun out of holster) You know what this is?
Cherry	A gun.

The Rapist	It's simplicity itself. You see, you point it at what you want to die. And you pull the little trigger here. And a little bullet comes outta here. (presses gun barrel against Cherry's cheek) And the little bullet...hits you right there! (indicates Cherry's forehead) And you know what? You don't look like Ava Gardner no more. (grabs her hair) Do not taunt me, tramp. I am not one to be taunted. Say 'I got it'. SAY 'I GOT IT'!
Cherry	I...got it. (Rapist turns elevator back on) (To herself) Tool.

Lyndon Morgans

Cold Coffee and Ava Gardner

She left some cargo-pants on the floor, said she won't be back any more.
There's a kid two gardens away been squawking 'Wonderwall' all day.

On my Betty Page centrefold, my cup of coffee's growing cold.
It's such a bleak place to be, this Alcatraz I call me.

She felt-tipped a message on my disco shoes,
'I could say I loved you, but it wouldn't be true.
You only wanted me 'cos I looked like Ava Gardner'...

Like in some French arthouse movie, all Chardonnay and ennui.
Still her touch felt like rain on my skin. Why don't that kid just pack it in?

I've got my cigarettes and my pills. I watch the sun dip over indigo hills.
Pick up her scent on a magazine, she's like some country I've never been.

She felt-tipped a message on my disco shoes,
'I could say I loved you, but it wouldn't be true.
You only wanted me 'cos I looked like Ava Gardner'...

Antony Owen

Ava Gardner
for Joanne Owen

Winter's prisoner
by plastic embers
Lamb hands held herself
as her mantelpiece son
smiles at her
from a forgotten beach
when she wrapped him in a towel
shivering that day.

Saturday brought David,
and a woman back to her.
He brought tangerines
combed her hair
whispering
"Mama,
you look like Ava Gardner."

Sunday brought her end,
though no one knew.
She died with a comb in her hand,
and when David found her
he wrapped her in a blanket
remembering that beach
when he shivered that day
in the arms of our Mama
by waves of "Porthtowan."

David Kirby

Strip Poker

I'm giving blood and looking at a magazine photo
of bosomy Ava Gardner next to that squirt Sinatra
and remembering saying, "Want to play strip poker?"
to my mom when I was eight because I thought it was a game,
not a way to get naked, and was ready to put on
lots of layers that hot July evening—
p.j.s, raincoat, my patrolboy's belt
with the badge I was so proud of—and figuring
my mom would do the same with her clothes:

the cotton dresses she taught fifth grade in
over the jeans and boots she wore for gardening
and, on top of everything, the long coat she wore
when she went out with my dad on cool nights
and the ratty mink stole her rich sister had given her.
My dad looked up from his newspaper, looked down again.
My mother looked up from her book, looked down again,
looked up again, said, "No, thank you, darling,"
which is how it was in our house:

no yelling, no explanation, even,
just the assumption that you were a smart kid,
you could figure things out on your own,
like "No, thanks" meant "no, but thank you anyway"
and not "zero thanks," or that the K-9 corps
was so-called because K-9 = canine,
i.e., wasn't just some arbitrary government code—
which is good, I guess, because if people
aren't constantly explaining stuff to you

when you're a kid, then you grow up mentally active,
though also doubting everything,
even yourself, because if you're the one
who comes up with the answers,
then what the hell good are they?
Which is the kind of thing that led
Kafka to ask, "What have I in common
with the Jews? I have hardly anything
in common with myself"

and might have led Stalin to ask,
"What have I in common with other human beings?"
only he was too busy coming up with rules
such as this one for the Union of Soviet Composers:
"The main attention of the Soviet composer
must be directed toward
the victorious progressive principles
of reality, toward all that is
heroic, bright, and beautiful."

But what about all
that is cowardly, dull, and ugly?
Tightrope-walker Karl Wallenda:
"To be on the wire is life;
the rest is waiting,"
only there's much more waiting than wire-walking,
so what are we supposed to do when we're on the ground?
Someone, not Henry James, I think, but one of those
Henry James kind of guys—cultured, reticent,

well-off but not too—said a gentleman
was a person who never knowingly made
anyone else uncomfortable, which is a good idea,
although one you can take too far,
because one of those smart old Greeks, maybe Sophocles,
said it was better never to be born,
and think how comfortable that would make everybody,
because if you weren't born, you couldn't bother anyone,

especially yourself!

"Are you a runner, Mr. Kirby?" asks Melba
the blood-bank nurse, who has two fingers
on my right wrist and one eye on her watch
and the other on me, who says,
no, he's not a runner, though he does a lot
of yard work, and why does she want to know,
and Melba says, "Because you have a pulse of 50,
and if you have a pulse of 50 and you're not a runner,
often that means you're dead,"

which, sooner or later,
I will be, will be naked again, sans p.j.s,
raincoat, belt and badge, everything.
The blood leaps from a vein in my elbow,
pools in a plastic sack, and I'm a little whiter
than I was when I read that Ava Gardner said,
"Deep down, I'm pretty superficial"—
deep down, Ava darling, we're all pretty superficial,
and beautiful, too, in or out of our clothes.

Peg Boyers

Family Portrait

Puerto La Cruz, 1956

It's the bland fifties but the news
has not reached Venezuela

where the bougainvillea and hibiscus
obscenely bloom.

In our backyard tropical oblivion
the family freezes for the photograph,

and for a millisecond captures falsity
for the record.

Even then you were uncomfortable
out of shadow.

At fourteen your manhood, just around
the corner, had yet to stake its claim.

The bare shoulder hunches up to involuntary rectitude.
Even at the beach your trained body slips

to attention. Your cocky squint
and Elvis sneer exude detached

experience, a ruse learned
at military school to bluff your wardens.

The tot (myself) on father's lap
is also detached.

Her eyes are only for you, Sweet Foreign Sibling,
Exotic American.

She reaches for your soldier hand,
but there's no reach back.

It's her first—and only—shot
at unrequited love, the earliest taste of exile.

Precocious pretty-boy flirt, little
homme fatal standing frigid—here, yet

away, alone—overexposed, uniformed
in braided blue, graduated, 'grown up,'

did you sense, then, what lay ahead?
Seduction and betrayal and then again the pitch,

a dynamic so familiar
it almost felt like home.

And then the biggest lie, the Saigon saga,
the drugs and drink to swallow it all.

The others pose for the camera,
competitive in their obedience,

but we, my still distant brother,
resist their matching Cheshire grins.

Our Ava Gardner mother flashes her Hollywood smile,
glamour-plated, seductive, calculating.

She leans over us, connects with the camera,
pulls us toward the lens with her greedy eyes.

Her husband, pasty-white, complicit
in a circle of offspring,

cradles the plump sweetness on his lap,
final issue of his fertile heart, while the others strain,

maintaining the flex of their cheeks—just so—
charming the available light.

Cheryl Clarke

Kitchen Mechanics Sequence

i.

D.C. was where we went to find work.
Mama could cook anything from possum to pheasant.
She loved a good time and a loud laugh.
She laughed at everyone and herself.
We was partners
and worked everywhere together.
Never let me take no live-in job.

Times always rough for poor folk
and every Thursday off was a starchy gravy.
Thursday night we took to the streets
and our separate ways.
Did not look over our shoulders.
Away from the white folks' houses
to the crowded, smoky, noisy joints
on U Street, the nigger strip.

Ran away with a gal one Thursday.
She got me a live-in job
out in Rosslyn
where she worked.
Me and her spent a whole month together
—late at night and real early.
Thursdays we took the streetcar
to her aunt's in Foggy Bottom
and onto evening
made our way to U Street.
It was on U Street Mama found me
and went up in my face and say:

"You may have to be a stud,
but you ain't gotta be no live-in slave."

That was the last time I did live-in work
or left Mama.
Nineteen then.
Been working since I was eight.

ii.
Every Thursday 6 o'clock
Mercy took me and Pru to the York Theatre.
There the three of us saw everything Hollywood made
then.
I was three when I saw *Mogambo*.
All I remember is Ava Gardner in the jungle singin
"Comin Through the Rye"
But Mercy...
her eyes froze to the screen
the minute the lights went out.
Thursday was her day
no matter what was showin.
Me and Pru sat through the double feature
trying to make our Jujy Fruits last.

Julia Lisella

Song of the Third Generation

I learned to read in the dark,
in the car, wherever the light
moved, shifted. My mother believed
I would burn my eyes out.
Between the breath and the text
my birth and hers kept happening
in the late night
in the daily horoscopes
in the 4:30 Movie
and the huge picture books filled with Hollywood stars.
My Ava Gardner died my mother says.
My mother learned how to read the text of a life
as her mother learned to translate *Il Progresso*:
by reading a bit of headline,
any little bit.
They could both predict disasters—my mother's
in American English: divorce, drug addiction
and insane asylums. Nonna's in Calabrian:
earthquakes earthquakes famine.
Somewhere between our mouths
and what we said is what we learned.
Somewhere in the old country
we breathed text
without knowing how to read.
I learned in the old way, too,
in a corner of the kitchen
watching my mother pour the batter
of flour and zucchini blossoms
into bright spattering oil,

or in the cool basement at the edge of the ironing board,
the lint speckling her dark sweater,
at her elbow as she whipped the cloth
beneath the needle of her industrial Singer.
No other record, no other text
exists but the buzzing and this way of learning
in the old way,
which is any way that we can.

Vivian Shipley

Sitting with My Grandmother,

Parealy Stewart Todd

Old stalks bleached from brown and pith dried, your fingers
can't peel or dry apples, hull or crack hickory nuts for jam cake.
Never thinking like Uncle Alonzo of how much tobacco could
fit in the back field, your vegetable garden was ploughed edge

to center, furrow to furrow squaring off as soil darkened under
weight of Snip's and Nellie's feet. That ground Grandpa fertilized
closed slowly, denting like dough you kneaded for the biscuits
I smeared with blackberry preserves scooped from green jars.

All broken now, like windows in your white house emptied
except for a velvet jacket hooked on a parlor door you wore on
your golden anniversary. At my touch, a bat I mistook for cloth
flew to hang on a sill. I would have brought it with me today,

but I was afraid there might be another bat, then another,
bunching like black walnuts with husks splitting for squirrels,
that quivered with hunger as I did at sixteen. Knowing thirst
work would quench, you'd wake me to hoe beans, scatter hens

that seemed to cluck: find a man, get married, have children.
There's nothing more. After Sunday services in Somerset,
I waited for a boy who wanted to take me behind the barn,
tongue my mouth, but you called me back. Frying chicken

came before sin. Grandpa had taught you breaking a mule
was mean business a girl didn't understand, even one like
Betty Grable looking over her shoulder in a white bathing suit.
Lord knows, Ava Gardner had tried. That was the year she met

Mickey Rooney. Mid-afternoon, you gave me the frosting
bowl as if licking brown sugar would fill me. I have crossed
off dirt roads from your map and marked interstates in red.
Why can't I drop your hand, plow you under like seed potato?

Briar Wood

The Ava Gardner House

Once, it was for sale,
but I was only eighteen.
A faithless then boyfriend
wanted to get married.

Turns out, it was a family place,
auctioned so that two brothers could
agree on a price. I imagine
Ava, post Frank, post matadors,

after Spain and before London,
writing to Lana, Grace and Bappie
because Hollywood gave them
and took away so much,

mixing mint julep on the veranda
in sarong and winged sunglasses
thinking of the future, barefoot,
making perfect gravy because

an actress is so much more than just
the sum of her parts, her arts. She'd be
reading about political economy
watching *West Wing* on tv,

babysitting, walking the dogs
along Mabel Thorburn Drive.
(Who was Mabel Thorburn?—
one of so many things I wish I knew.)

This place has changed since her heyday.
The oak tree's been chopped down
on what was the site of Mangonui's
first hotel, the Donnybrook,

(Ava would appreciate the redundancy
of cliché) built in 1842, burnt down,
replaced by the Settlers Arms Hotel
in 1873, demolished 1906.

But a blazon of yellow hibiscus is there
in the pond shaped concrete garden,
and with fifties deco composure Bay View
looks out across the still yachts in Mill Bay.

Cheryl Diane Kidder

December, 1989, San Francisco

from "Beds"

LOTS OF BLOND HAIR. Ten, maybe fifteen years younger than me. Mattress on the floor of his room in the Haight. His room smaller than the closet in my studio up on Leavenworth. Every inch of wall space covered with posters and articles and record jackets. Only a stereo and the bed. Lights on, too bright, too much information, couldn't take it all in. Lights out, sit down on the bed, too close to the floor. Close my eyes. Beer buzzing in my head.

I hear the zipper on my dress being unzipped in the back. Nice vintage dress—an Ava Gardner dress, worked well for me. He sat cross-legged in front of me and pulled it down to my waist. I rolled my head back and smiled. Fucking Damien, the boss's son. Not out of jail for a week and he's already back into it. I'd always wondered about him: cute little punk would always steal money out of the front register, we'd write up slips of paper and charge them to his dad. He'd thrown my new black bra somewhere now and unzipped his pants. Damn, this was just what I needed, a huge thick dick right in front of me and me barely able to keep my eyes open. He put his hand on the back of my neck. I closed my eyes and thought of popsicles and ice cream cones and all the years I'd chased him out of the back room when I was counting out the drawers.

William Corbett

Gerald at Sixty-Seven

First, your lungs
And breathing. Asthma
Colored you gray
Like cigarette ash.
Now your jawbone,
Five posts for five
Implants in five months.
Lucky you to live
By eye and ear,
New Sicilian collages
And Fauré, Franck,
Saint-Saëns through
The birthday you share
With Cher Maître Proust.
Sixty-seven! How pure
Are numbers. They mean
Nothing like winters
Or summers. Everyone
Forgets dates but
Remembers Proust abed
Then starting at that
Apple tree in flower.

He had himself driven
To it, nightshirt
Under his overcoat.
He remembered what
He wanted to see;
He had to look
Hard to see it, bright
World's wedding dress.
That's the perfect Proust

90

Gerald of Battenville,
And you're perfectly you
Eyes peeled, drawing
Trees leaved and bare
Beside and above
Your shallow Battenkill
Or collaging sexy Ava
In her fuck me mules.
You with fresh teeth
And breath enough
To carry you again
To Palermo and thru!

Gerald's Ava born
A Tarheel, rusted
Spoon in her mouth.
Ava, walking wet dream
That cleft in her chin!
She hit the daily double:
Frank Sinatra, Mickey Rooney.
No! Trifecta! Artie Shaw.

Oh, those ballistic tits!
High school trouser raisers
To fall on them and die!
Near sighted Contessa Ava
Ole'd the ring through our nose
Who wouldn't let her shit
On his chest and dance in it.

Main Line's Grace
Grabtown's Lucy Johnson
Hot for small men
Liked their matinees
The one blonde ice
Her panties on fire
The other Latin tempered
Cheap but not coarse

Out of central casting
to launch 10,000 ships
The ocean's roar, jungle drums...
Close the cave door
Back to Pygmy country!

It's the fan
An insect wing
Her innocence, to act
Sexy Vulnerable
Spanish Indian
Ever the Ava
Of our innocent
Imaginings, pure
Unreachable star,
Come hither lips
Parted, small voice
Untrained...what
Would Almodovar
Lover of women
Have done with her?

Walker Joe Jackson

The Last Eight Bars

from Francis Albert Sinatra

While dancing downtown, swinging Turner around,
Who should Frank meet, so sassy and neat?
Miss Ava Gardner. Howard Hughes was her partner.
But not for long, 'cause Frank came on strong.

Ava! Ava! Mama! Mama!
A red haired goddess who was slightly modest.
With feline eyes that hypnotized and tantalized.
Frank's body and soul, and his world as a whole.

Pere Gimferrer

from La Muerte en Beverly Hills

v.

En las cabinas telefónicas
hay misteriosas inscripciones dibujadas con lápiz de labios.
Son las últimas palabras de las dulces muchachas rubias
que con el escote ensangrentado se refugian allí para morir.
Última noche bajo el pálido neón, último día bajo el sol alucinante,
calles recién regadas con magnolias, faros amarillentos de
los coches patrulla en el amanecer.
Te esperaré a la una y media, cuando salgas del cine—y a
esta hora está muerta en el Depósito aquélla cuyo
cuerpo era un ramo de orquídeas.
Herida en los tiroteos nocturnos, acorralada en las esquinas
por los reflectores, abofeteada en los night-clubs,
mi verdadero y dulce amor llora en mis brazos.
Una última claridad, la más delgada y nítida,
parece deslizarse de los locales cerrados:
esta luz que detiene a los transeúntes
y les habla suavemente de su infancia.
Músicas de otro tiempo, canción al compás de cuyas viejas
notas conocimos una noche a Ava Gardner,
muchacha envuelta en un impermeable claro que besamos
una vez en el ascensor, a oscuras entre dos pisos, y
tenía los ojos muy azules, y hablaba siempre en voz
muy baja—se llamaba Nelly.
Cierra los ojos y escucha el canto de las sirenas en la noche
plateada de anuncios luminosos.
La noche tiene cálidas avenidas azules.
Sombras abrazan sombras en piscinas y bares.
En el oscuro cielo combatían los astros
cuando murió de amor,
y era como si oliera muy despacio un perfume.

Pere Gimferrer

from Death in Beverly Hills

translated by Paloma LaPuerta and Ninon Larché
v.

In phone booths
there are mysterious messages penned in lipstick.
Last words of the sweet young blondes
who with bloody cleavage sought refuge here to die.
One last night under the pallid neon, one last day beneath a frenzied sun,
wet streets recently scattered with magnolias, yellow headlights of
patrol cars at daybreak.
I'll be waiting for you at half past one, when the film is over—
and at that hour she is already dead in the Morgue,
she whose body was once a spray of orchids.
Wounded in nocturnal gunfire, trapped at intersections
by spotlights, slapped about in nightclubs,
my sweet, true love cries in my arms.
A last ray of light, the thinnest, sharpest,
seems to stream out of closed joints:
a light which stops onlookers
and gently speaks to them of their childhood.
Melodies of another time, a song to whose old notes
one night, we met Ava Gardner,
a young woman wrapped in a light raincoat whom we kissed
once, in the elevator, in the darkness between two floors, and
her eyes were very blue, and her voice was
always soft– her name was Nelly.
She closes her eyes and listens to the song of sirens in the night
turned silvery under the flashing billboards.
There are warm blue boulevards in the night,
shadows embracing shadows in pools and bars
In dark skies the stars were fighting
when she died of love,
and it was like smelling a perfume very slowly.

Alain Souchon

La Beauté d'Ava Gardner

J'aime les hommes qui sont c'qu'ils peuvent
Assis sur le bord des fleuves
Ils regardent s'en aller dans la mer
Les bouts de bois les vieilles affaires
La beauté d'Ava Gardner

Ca met dans leurs yeux un air
De savoir que tout va dans la mer
La jeune fille adoucie des soirs de verre
Les bateaux les avions de guerre
La beauté d'Ava Gardner

Les murs écroulés du monde
Filez nos belles enfances blondes
Edith Nylon les nageuses a l'envers
Les odeurs dans les chemins de fer
La beauté d'Ava Gardner

J'aime les regretteurs d'hier
Qui trouvent que tout ce qu'on gagne on le perd
Qui voudraient le cours des rivières
Retrouver dans la lumière
La beauté d'Ava Gardner
Retrouver les choses premières
La beauté d'Ava Gardner

Alain Souchon

The Beauty of Ava Gardner

translated by Laurence Petit and Pascal Bataillard

I like men who are what they can
Sitting on river banks
Watching driftwood and old things
Flowing away to the sea
The beauty of Ava Gardner

It gives their eyes a certain air
To know that everything ends in the sea
The languid girl of drunken nights
The ships and war planes
The beauty of Ava Gardner

The tumbled walls of the world
Begone our golden childhood years
Edith Nylon girls swimming backwards
The smells on trains
The beauty of Ava Gardner

I like men who regret the past
And believe that all we gain we lose
Men who wish to retrieve in the light
The courses of rivers
The beauty of Ava Gardner
To retrieve primeval things
The beauty of Ava Gardner

Mario Cabré

El Diccionario

—*Please, give me the dictionary, I will talk to you.*

—El diccionario guarda
la sombra escalonada
de las palabras.

Mas no mi angustia de felicidad.

El pulmón de las páginas
en la búsqueda ensancha
su voz callada.

Mi silencio respira enamorado
y dice mucho más.

La expresión en su túnica
aparece desnuda,
fría y oscura,

La que surge en mis seines encendidas
empieza en un soñar.

Aquí, la mar es muda.
El amor no se inmuta.
La vida oculta.

Por favor, cierra el diccionario
y mírame tan sólo.

Gerona, 3 mayo
Miércoles mañana.

Mario Cabré

The Dictionary

translated by Katherine Sugg

—*Please, give me the dictionary, I will talk to you.*

—The dictionary holds
the staggered shadow
of my words.

I no longer suffer from happiness.

The breathless pulse of pages
Expands the search
For her silenced voice.

My silence breathes only love
And says much more.

The expression in her gown
Appears naked,
Cold and dark.

What pulses in my fiery veins
Begins the dreaming.

Here, the sea is mute.
Love does not change.
Life conceals.

Please, close the dictionary,
And look at me so alone

Gerona, May 3
Wednesday morning

Michael O'Leary

from It's Not the Leaving of Wellington
for Moana

viii.

Along the spaghetti highway or pasta
Main vibrato rail to the Hutt Valley
We travel, reaching the rundown grandeur
Of Petone Railway Station which branches out
To Melling, or on to the main suburban route

Where the Ava gardener tends his plot
And skinhead graffiti offers threats
Black thoughts caught in crazy bald heads
Then the train turns sharply to the left to
Cross the river and meet its Waterloo

Past Pomare, son of another waiata aroha
To count the cars on the Silverstream
Turnpike, we've come to look for another car
In a triumph of British engineering skill
The Irish Rover takes us over Haywards Hill

Down into the Porirua Basin we drive
Then, pushing the supermarket trolley, we
Count down the days and many hours
When we will live in our Hacienda by the sea
Our Spanish daze shimmering in Paekakariki

Where we live and love and play with shells
And land and sea creatures of many hues
Where we swim, and you take Dogwog walking
And, driving up the Paraparaumu mini-golf range
Or, on the evening verandah watching sunsets change

Things move on, we no longer live under
The same roof, yet our lives still intertwine
Along a line of towns from Tawa to the crossing
Of McKays. It's not the leaving of Wellington
But the love lines which connect us on and on

Yorgos Ioannou

Mrs. Minotaur

translated by Peter Mackridge and Jackie Willcox

MRS. ARIADNE MINOTAUR was in a black mood that day. The fact is that she was seldom in a bright mood besides, she vastly preferred a black mood—but that New Year's Day she was in a blacker-than-black mood. And yet the poor trollop had done everything to make that particular day, the first day of the new year, as bright as a button, as bright as newly-washed linen. Good sorceress that she was, she had tried to achieve this by means of homoeopathy. She had got hold of a huge black aubergine, on which she had spat and made the sign of the cross, then licked it, caressed it and oiled it, and at the precise moment that the new year was beginning and the hooting of the taxis in Unwed Square—so named because it used to be the haunt of those who were looking for partners—sounded in her ears like gipsy violins, she shouted the signal, "Come and get your victuals, kids!", which was calculated to arouse already aroused appetites.

"Fiddlesticks!" cried the soldier when he heard the noble signal, his response being clearly well-intentioned, since they were by now old friends, having known each other two whole hours—in fact, they were like brother and sister. How right the old books are, thought the idealistic Ariadne once she had got over her initial difficulties and felt a bit better: "Verily, a sister aided by a brother is like a fortress."

Now Ariadne was popping in and out of her little kitchen, preparing the New Year sweetmeats and asking her new friend, who was the dearest thing in the world to her, what he liked to eat. She was of course wearing that worn, aubergine-coloured house-coat of hers that had become famous throughout Greece since that black day on the underground when she had accosted two youths, whose ambition, as it turned out, was to become airmen, and without more ado inveigled them with vague promises into her semi-basement flat.

Another of her famous mottos was, "In a flash have a bash." So, true to her principles, she took them home in a flash and after putting on her house-coat, which hadn't been washed since the heroic days of Madame Hortense in Kazantzakis' *Zorba the Greek*, she came demurely out of the privy—she had no bath at her place, only a shower, and there's nothing wrong with that. But she fancied herself like the Queen of Sheba since she was the mistress of Savva the footballer, whom she would address as "my lover" in front of her friends, practically causing him to have a heart-attack.

The would-be airmen—and lovers—were shocked by the sight of this phenomenon now they saw it wearing a dress. What an ugly sight! Her eyes were distended and bloodshot—a cross between "owl-eyed" and "dog-eyed"—, her pointed ears projected from her bald round skull, her mouth was huge and always smeared with vaseline, she stood no more than one metre fifty, and she swung her hips like nobody's business.

She came out of the privy, where she had given herself an enema, prepared in complete accordance with the health regulations. "Ava Gardner! I'm Ava Gardner!" she announced to them, rocking from side to side. Not even Ava Gardner's stillborn foetus would have looked like this.

The would-be airmen drew back. "How much will you give us?" they asked her directly. She began talking in riddles in an attempt to confuse them. That's how she always was—avoiding any prior agreement and then trapping them. You'll give us such-and-such an amount, they told her. What bastards these were, country bumpkins determined to get rich quick. The smile froze on Ariadne's lips. "I shall give you my body," she said. "Your body? You brought us back here to give us your body?" the bastards began to mutter. "Come on, either hand over the dosh or we'll take your clock." It was a cheap clock, but in those days even a cheap clock was a luxury item in a working-class home. Ariadne, belligerent, spiteful and stupid as she was, lunged to stop them. They gave her a hefty shove and grabbed the clock. "I know who you are; I'll go to the police!" she shouted after them down the corridor.

She was still wandering about the flat in her housecoat, shaking with rage, when there was a ring at her doorbell. There was a policeman standing there—and what a nice one! Ariadne fluffed herself up. "A customer," she thought, "and just in time!" "Mrs. Ariadne Minotaur?" asked the policeman politely. Ariadne wrapped her house-coat tightly round her skinny frame to show how slender and happy she was. "In person!" she whispered. "Come in!" But the policeman neither smiled nor went in. "Get dressed quickly," he told her. "We're going down to the station." So Ariadne got dressed, all the time playing the innocent, while the great hunk of a policeman played the innocent too.

At the station, naturally, she found herself face to face with the two airmen, who had taken fright at her threat, left the clock somewhere, and hurried to get to the police first. They claimed she had inveigled them, changed into a dress in order to seduce them, kept waggling her hips as she got undressed, made filthy comments, and tried to grab them "there," whereupon they rebelled and ran off, pushing her aside. The bastards had cunningly covered up the struggle over the clock so that they could justify any scratches that might be found on them. "But why did you go with him, if you didn't want it?" asked the inspector. "He duped us by inviting us for a drink," said the bastards with feigned naivete.

Wily as she was, Ariadne was dumbstruck. She had had a higher opinion of "men"; she had thought them more honest and artless. "So you found these innocent creatures, took them home, put on a dress and made advances to them," said the inspector sharply. "But it wasn't a dress, it was my house-coat." "It's the same thing," replied the inspector, and ordered his fingerprints to be taken. After this they got him to sign his statement and packed him off home with gleeful sneers. The main thing was that the detail about the dress even reached the court.

So she was popping in and out of her little kitchen in her historic house-coat, asking Bessaris from Kalambaka what he liked to eat, when suddenly the doorbell rang. It was that poor friend of hers, Ruhi.

Ruhi, the Star of the Orient was her full stage-name, but she was called Ruhi for short. It was an Indian name— probably Sanskrit— taken from a cheap Indian movie. She had gone to see it regularly so as to find some likely lads among the simple but strapping pariahs from the working-class areas, and since it was on for at least three weeks the nickname stuck. It was Ruhi that Ariadne had gone down to Omonia Square with on New Year's Eve. But as they were cruising around about ten o'clock they came upon Bessaris, who was walking alone, whereupon Ariadne grabbed him excitedly and bundled him into a taxi, shouting to the astonished Ruhi, "Come in two hours!"

And so poor Ruhi, who had declined invitations to various salons in order to accompany the apparently forlorn Ariadne, began roaming the night streets like a stray dog. "The cow! The randy old sow!" she thought as she walked. Finally, unable to go on wandering the desolate streets where nobody took any notice of her, she went home, where she listened to all the hooting and the fireworks with tears in her eyes. It was the start of the 60s. Later she found out that Bessaris was entering his Bessarabia at precisely that moment.

But how could Ruhi stay at home any longer? All her New Year shopping—all her food and drink—was at Ariadne's. They had gone to the grocer's and the butcher's in plenty of time, and by the time they were finished they had collected four basketfuls. Ariadne was skint as usual. So Ruhi—provident Ruhi, Star of the Orient—paid for everything. They planned to have a ball: plenty of food and drink, singing, and a dance or two from Ariadne, who—bless her!—was a mean dancer, and if they found a couple of lads, then so much the better. In her heart of hearts Ruhi hoped that Ariadne would sing some arias. When she first heard her she laughed so much that she fell off her chair.

So Ariadne came to the door wearing her house-coat and slippers. She held up her hand like a policeman stopping the traffic and said with a bitchy smile, "Bessaris doesn't want anybody else. Come back tomorrow morning and give me another hand—I've already had one hand tonight! Happy New Year, darling!" Poor Ruhi stood there like a pillar of salt. She had no time to mention her provisions, her drinks and her presents, which the unsuspecting Bessaris was now enjoying. She went off again, and the pavement was dampened by her tender tears.

Nevertheless, since she had nothing better to do, she went back to Ariadne's first thing in the morning. She had an ulterior motive, because she wanted to see how far this business would go. She had paid her fees and she wanted to learn.

Ariadne was in her house-coat, sweeping up and looking irritated. She was giving Bessaris a good scolding. "It's the same old story," thought Ruhi. Bessaris had tripped over the wire of a ridiculous bedside lamp and brought it crashing to the ground. The way Ariadne was mumbling to herself as she swept, the beefcake thought he had broken a Sèvres vase. "That's just what she wanted," thought Ruhi, whose eyes had completely opened by now. "Now she'll try to get out of paying." "You'll have to pay me for it!" Ariadne started shrieking. Bessaris got dressed in embarrassment, made straight for the door and went out. Ariadne stopped sweeping immediately. She took off her housecoat, got dressed, put on a little rouge and said, "It's a lovely day today. Shall we go to the Royal Gardens?" And they went off without more ado.

First they went by the Tomb of the Unknown Soldier but found nothing there, not even a handsome sentry. There were just a lot of kids enjoying the January sunshine. "How disgusting they are!" snorted Ariadne. Ruhi made bold to point out that they would grow up one day, but Ariadne, a maiden of at least fifty summers, retorted angrily with Kazantzakis' watchword, "I hope for nothing; I fear nothing; I am free—free and beautiful!" "Hark at her!" shouted an itinerant peanut-seller. "Piss off, you faggot!" responded Ariadne. "Who are you calling a faggot, you old queen?" Ripples of laughter spread around them. "Let's go!" said Ruhi, dragging her off. But Ariadne remained oblivious. She got caught up with some gays who were laughing a bit too loudly. "Faggots!" she shouted at them, waggling her hips, while they split their sides laughing but said nothing. The nerve of this wiggle-arse was quite unbelievable, calling everyone else a faggot. "And what are you, then?" they asked eventually. "I am a man with special tastes!" she replied haughtily.

At that point pandemonium broke out. Everyone was rolling around laughing. The man with special tastes walked away with his head held high. "Bloody queers!" people were shouting at them. Ruhi, who had been trying to keep her distance, caught up with her and dragged her off out of harm's way. "Let's go to the Royal Gardens. There's nothing for us here."

They entered the gardens from Vasilissis Sophias Avenue and made straight for the pond with its black, gold and white fish. They aimed to look around for some talent. A soldier was sitting sunning himself on one of the benches. The rest were empty. Ariadne immediately abandoned Ruhi and sat down on the bench next to the soldier. Anyone who came along would be sure to notice them.

But Ariadne, who was incurably provincial and would never have left her village if the partisans hadn't decided to hunt her down because of her intimate relations with the Germans—from those experiences she had retained a little German but, more importantly, a fathomless hatred for anything remotely associated with the Left, like a left foot for instance—had no sense of the capital, nor was she likely to attain one. She believed that since she couldn't find her way through all this jungle, nobody else could either. But the soldier was no less of a peasant, and very soon Ruhi saw them get up and start walking away. They had made a deal.

"Come back in an hour," Ariadne gestured to her. And indeed, an hour later, the obedient and long-suffering Ruhi was ringing Mrs. Minotaur's doorbell. But now she knew more or less what she would find, and she was determined to plumb the depths of Ariadne's shameless dishonesty. They had finished, naturally, and Ariadne had once more found an excuse to stomp about in a rage. Ruhi sat down in trepidation; the tension was running high. "What's the matter?" she asked. "Mrs. Ariadne's refusing to pay me like we agreed," replied the soldier in a humble voice. "What a coincidence!" thought Ruhi, but said nothing.

Ariadne came out of the lavatory, where she was mopping up some water. "I told you to wait, didn't I?" she shouted in a frenzy. "Why were you in such a hurry? Just look at all this water you've spilt!" "What a bawdy-house," thought Ruhi. "I've never witnessed such a filthy row." She looked at the huge soldier. "Why don't you wring her neck? I'll be a witness that you were provoked and you did it in the heat of the moment." But the poor soldier sat there shamefaced in the hope that the reptilian Ariadne would take pity on him and hand over the agreed fifty drachmas. "Go on, lad, lose your temper!" But he did nothing.

In the end Ariadne put her hand into the pocket of her house-coat and brought out a small note— no more than ten drachmas—and gave it angrily to the soldier. "That's for your cigarettes!" The soldier disappeared. "Phew!" exclaimed Ariadne. "What a filthy creature. He couldn't even wait for me! How do they expect to get married in their state?"

By now it was noon. Mrs. Minotaur generously offered to bring out the leftovers of the food that Ruhi had bought for her. She brought them out with trembling hands, as though she fancied she was performing a great act of charity for a poor famished, homeless creature. Ruhi felt indignant. "The mean bitch!" She saw clearly that the ravenous Ariadne had appropriated Ruhi's food from the moment she had bought it.

Later, when Ruhi got to know more elderly working-class marchionesses, she found that Ariadne's personality wasn't unique. All of them skinflints who made a great pretence of generosity. They were completely lacking in self-awareness. "All I want is to meet one who's well-balanced," she would say. Suddenly Ruhi stopped chewing. "Aria, what does Unwed Square mean?" "I'm Unwed Square," declared Ariadne complacently. " But unless I'm mistaken you're not unwed." "Of course I'm not unwed—I'm Unwed Square, I tell you. The unwed enter the square—and I'm the square." "What's going to happen now they've renamed it America Square?" "It'll be discovered by Columbus and his crew." She was indefatigable.

Eventually Ruhi decided to leave, since the shades of night were falling fast. She wanted to find something for herself; she was fed up with being at the beck and call of Ariadne, who, old and ugly as she was, constantly acted like someone whose days were numbered. "I want this, I want that, and I want the other too!" Just like a baby.

As she went outside she caught sight of two soldiers in the park. And what soldiers they were! They were in the royal horseguards, and they had a capital F on their epaulettes, the initial of Queen Frederika. They turned round to look when she opened the door. She felt like a celebrity until she realized it was in Ariadne's honour that they had turned round. She turned tail and told Ariadne all about it.

Curiously enough, Ariadne showed great magnanimity. "Wait here," she said, "and I'll introduce you to one of them." She gathered her house-coat round her, half-opened the door and beckoned. The soldiers immediately came downstairs, and the flat was filled with male bodies. Ariadne knew one of them already; she took the new one into the closet.

After a while she announced she would go with the new one. But in looks he wasn't a patch on the other, a brave fellow from Roumeli. It was the first time Ruhi had accepted Ariadne's proposal. "What a fantastic arrangement! She's isn't like I thought she was. But then why was she in such a frenzy over that one last night? I just can't fathom her." Ariadne withdrew and left them alone, whereupon a great commotion ensued. Eventually they all met up again, and the moment of truth drew near. Ruhi waited to see what excuse Ariadne would cook up to get out of paying.

The horsemen were sitting there comfortably and expectantly. Things weren't at all easy now. Ariadne called Ruhi into the hall. "Lend me a couple of hundred, will you?" she asked. Ruhi suddenly realized why Ariadne had kept her there. And so she "lent" her the money, and the problem was solved at her expense. "To hell with her!" she thought. "Filthy bitch! A man with special tastes indeed!" The soldiers pocketed a hundred each and made off. Now that Ruhi had become a victim of her own gullibility, she had neither the money nor the inclination to go out. "Stay here," said Ariadne. "Savva's coming with his mates—all footballers."

Sure enough, in the early evening half a dozen colourless creatures turned up; the much-vaunted Savva was the worst of the lot. "What bad taste she has!" Ruhi was afraid she might be forced to keep company with them, but her fears were groundless. The men sat round the table and began earnestly playing cards without even so much as a glance at her and Ariadne. It was pitiful to see Ariadne constantly bringing drinks, glasses of water, nuts and other snacks to those brutes, who never bothered to say thank you.

Ruhi reclined on a divan, reading; there wasn't a chair for her to sit on. Having dropped off to sleep at one point, she felt a hand stroking her groin. "Ah, the footballers at last!" she thought as she emerged from her torpor. It wasn't of course the footballers, but Ariadne playing a joke. She had done it once before in a cinema queue, and it was actually very funny. As Ruhi was standing there, she felt someone fondling her buttocks. She turned round surreptitiously to look and saw Ariadne's satanic smile as she disappeared into the crowd. At long last the footballers cleared off, but they left an awful fug behind them, together with a pile of rubbish, cigarette-ends and caked mud. Ruhi got up to help. Being a bit of a poet, she recited some apposite verses:

> The Turks only stayed a little while,
> But they left poor Chios a desert isle.

"Why are you blaming the poor lads?" asked Ariadne, swearing at her. Like all establishments with high principles, Ariadne believed the customer was always right. She also applied the rigid principle that "no mistakes can be rectified after the customer leaves the till." The till was her Achilles' heel—well, not her heel exactly, but some other Achillean part of her shriveled body. "Haven't I got sylph-like legs!" she would sometimes exclaim, showing off her bony shanks with the skin hanging off them.

What ox-eyed Ruhi couldn't understand was how such fresh-faced lads could go with dog-eyed Ariadne. "Don't they look at her?" she wondered. "Can't they see those rotten teeth, swollen gums and bald pate, those dewlaps hanging from her neck, those staring, bloodshot eyes, that poisonous malice and weasely cunning of hers?" And so Ruhi resigned herself never to boast about any conquest, since they simply didn't take any notice. They just wanted to get rid of their frustrations and be able to boast that, as men, they had something special, and they would go with the first person who came along. "Aria, what does it mean to say you've got fire in your belly?" "Me, I've got fire in my belly" replied Ariadne boastfully. "Aren't you afraid you might burn them?"

They went to sleep late and alone, two lonely maidens, Ariadne in the room next to the street and Ruhi on the inside near the hall. At about three in the morning they were awoken by some violent knocks, or rather kicks, on the shutters. It had to be kicks, since even the politest of men couldn't knock on the basement window except with his feet.

And indeed it was the politest, namely Markos, a Greek airman from Alexandria. Ariadne, keeping the shutter closed, opened the window and asked who it was. Markos asked her to open up in French, if you please. He knew that Ariadne loved to play the linguist. But tonight she wasn't having any of it. Since her French wasn't good enough for a real argument, she addressed her harridan's shouts to him in the local dialect. "Clear off at once! Nice boys don't roam the streets at this hour!" The words sounded odd in the mouth of that scrubber Ariadne. Ruhi knew the real reason, though—Ariadne didn't fancy him because of his small dimensions, and the only reason why she kept up relations with him was so as to practice her French, which Markos spoke so beautifully.

Ariadne put on her house-coat and went out muttering. A gradually mounting argument was resounding in the corridor, Markos shouting in French and Ariadne in her own version of the parley-voo. Finally Ariadne's tragic cry rose into the night. "*Je n'ai pas d'argent! Je n'ai pas d'argent!*" she howled, beating her breast. She was now shouting in French into the desolate night the words that she had refused even to whisper in Greek. It was the first time that Ruhi had heard Ariadne telling the truth so passionately.

But when doors began to open and angry, drowsy voices began to be heard, Ariadne had no option but to bundle Markos into the basement. "That's where you're going to sleep," she said sternly, pointing at an armchair and casting an immobilizing glance at Ruhi, who was ready to go home so as to make space for Markos on the divan. And indeed, as soon as she heard Ariadne's gentle snoring again, she did just that.

She dressed silently, placed a coin in Markos' hand and, waving goodbye to him, slipped outside into the enchantment of the piercingly cold January night. "I think I'll pop down to Omonia Square for a yoghurt," she thought. Then she whispered, "I won't be going back there in a hurry!" And, hoisting her white sails, she steered a course towards the glorious square: "Ariadne Minotaur kaput!"

Roxanne Fontana

America – Whore of Babylon – Mars, Mars, Mars

Northern Italy, June 2006

Face it, yes—
I'm typing this on a Swedish typewriter from another time: Face it—
in script
was this made for chicks?
Intellectual Swede moon blood, right NOW,
or, once upon a time…

The last time I said goodbye to my parents
45th Street—new times square, in front of old Johnnies.
much happened there—I was rich.
The biggest bags of greatness herbal,
perfumed my world…
& I slept with an impotent rapist…
& my most favourite cat, of 16 ¾ years,
shook out his final breath defiantly. Sun square sun.
I kissed red boy there the first time too,
102 fever, December.
It was the day after the big snow storm, and yes,
the night after the love is blue show at cbs gallery…
where
spitting gobs of green hell that some demon laughingly
spewed in my lungs, thank you,
in that hall on 45th Street, and later, that week before,
at the 10th Street Baths,
where I've seen Lou Reed disappear,
cockroach heaven. Sun square sun.
west 45th Street, here I was again.
The last time I said goodbye to my parents.
waving final waves - spring sun…

them, me, red boy, little red girl—
my mother of the fascist roman catholic dream.
I told her she was "on her own now," disgusted,
but now it was me.
West 45th Street squinting in the April sun, the five of us…
Johnnies, closed and shut away, forever more…
but before us there was Frank and Ava,
the big tub, rub rub—I twirled in their tub
thick old Italian marble wall.
The lady from the village voice told me I should cut it out of the wall
and take it,
if I ever leave.
The low red carpeted ceiling downstairs,
it flaked off in your fingers at the touch
& here it was, Dean Martin's lungs—
everybody falls in love somehow.

Italia, Castellaro, is where I am now
not too far from vive la france & not close enough.
Up a hill of many mountains, behind a gate
and a video screen,
suffocating.
In a room paneled as a coffin—
some old kraut woman with the worst artistic taste— dead today
but her shit remains, cramping my soul.
Inge Borg Hochwald. the people in the village say she was a fat miser—
respect the dead.

Los Angeles, California—
that was the city…
I called there twice now in two weeks
throw the phone in horror.
I had to get away…
oh is its lameness even worth words?
That last night, starving & wretched
and then vomiting on my favorite food…
Would I escape? And what?
The phonies who serve two masters—

medicated crippled sad crying drowning
or
blatantly living the lie, it
all leads to The Crack.
Break crack—
the world's biggest & most famous crypt
opening up like some colorful medieval book of hours
tapestry
only today.
Deep wide shaking shattering tumble
rumble—I see the earth open
5.6, 6.5, 9.7—very dry death
scum & stupidity
barren of all art and inspiration, finally, yet once a fountain
spring
but rot potential was ever present as
the warning.
respect the dead?

America with your 1950's Las Vegas A-bomb parties at dawn,
you knew it would lead to this—
whore of babylon, (that's)
Iraq, America whore of babylon.

Pigs of the earth from the pig farm,
how on earth did it ever come to this...
all-of-a-sudden.
everyone saw it coming, they said,
then no one looked and it happened.
Frozen gun metal freezer in the hot texas sun.
cia. lsd. manchurian candidate.
neil bush.
two tabs for two texas boys
david hinkley / marc d chapman
weeks apart pop pop
pop pop pop pop
one lived the other didn't.
someone told me

lennon sang in the beautiful people song:
"Baby, you're a rich, fat jew." Allen Klein.
sam cooke, brian jones - respect the dead.
here we were, bombing the garden of eden, after
the bombing of the capitalists in wall street:
high up, glassed in,
no air, no green,
no life.
flammable powdered milk in bad morning coffee
and a planes nose.

America whore of babylon, I am so glad I am
"out of you" today, for I believe in the Holy Ghost
and the good book, it says,
come out of her.
Aztecian day dream—dream the day away
2012—
next year we sing that David Bowie song,
it's all we got.
It's all over, 2012, with the shouting.
Trumpets blare, after
2 ½ years of total shit, after
the destruction of the whore…

I love to sleep with red boy, all entwined legs, where
you don't know whose leg is whose, and all the who in whoville…
under the Italian sun,
with the English rain—outside,
in the New York filth,
as the L.A. cop-ters chop,
we are aeons apart and
so together, with red girl.
poor red boy, he says,
"but it's ALWAYS been like this."
but I know different.

David Miller

Drunk Talking to No One

That's the politics baby—
you're that black boy they shot up
down on 1-4-9 street. You
come running out of the building
fast like you got jets on your feet.
Running just to be running
and the blue coats in the heat
of "hot pursuit" took you down.
Ain't young no more, think on that
before you talk 'bout how bad
the old days was. Like me
and crazy like a fox too.
All them fancy Johns and Janes
lived up Sugar hill and we,
me and my brothers stayed out
late to see them. It was something,
and cost nothing but a few
bruises on the behind, never had
much use for sitting no how.
Men wore shiny conks their suits
pressed sharp like they'd been folded
from the good paper white folks wrote on.
Women in sparkling off-the-shoulder
dresses that come in close and smooth
'round the hips, set me to thinking
on the life of a dress. Oh yes,
boy they had it made and how
Ava Gardner and Cary Grant
had nothing on them. But I
was a boy like you; didn't know

them black folks miles above me
was still under the same heel
of the same big shoe that ground
Malcolm and Martin and Medgar
to dirt, the same heel that followed
me around downtown stores or
tripped me up on the way to school.
You know what I mean boy, don't
say you don't cause I see some prints
on you. Bloody prints that iced
over them fancy-footwork
feet. I would'a told ya, if I'd
known this was your marked day,
to sit tight in a corner and pray
they let you slide. But it
might'a come some other how
and you'd been hiding stead of running
which is the way you're best,
besides, young as you were you
couldn't have done nothing too wrong.
Probably you'll find a mama
gone ahead of her children
who has some extra lovin' and
a lap you can dream from of how it would've been
if you hadn't stopped—just then

Michael S. Harper

Sinatra (1915 - 1998)

My father, born in the same year,
went to his own handmade cassette tape

when he heard the news: Cedars
never got over Ava Gardner

Maggio a hit because of Clift
the twin shadows of Hawaiian shirts

in the bombing of animal tension
song of the saloon of Jack Daniels

and mean even in the color scheme
of Las Vegas until he held the line

against segregation, Hoboken calm;
Palm Springs has a water fountain

in the waterline of Pal Joey
candidate Manchurian as he switched

allegiance in a dark suit Palladium
as the sox of Paramount took orders

took places where Riddle Basie were Capitol
in labels supreme as you drift into bites

of irony, afterglow, a scant frame
at the edge of conquistadorial defeat

c-notes of understanding
of how to win when up against the wall, always

Tom Russell

When Sinatra Played Juarez

Uncle Tommy Gabriel, he played the blue piano,
while Frank and Ava Gardner danced the wild Juarenzic tango.
"Those were truly golden years," my Uncle Tommy says,
"but everything's gone straight to hell since Sinatra played Juarez."

"I wish life was still like that," my Uncle Tommy says,
"but everything's gone straight to hell since Sinatra played Juarez.
You could get a cheap divorce, get your Pontiac tuck and rolled;
you could take your dolly to the dog track in her fake chinchilla stole."

"The Fiesta Club, The Chinese Palace, The Old Kentucky Bar
the matadors and baseball heroes and great big movie stars.
Those were truly golden years," my Uncle Tommy says,
"'cause everything's gone straight to hell since Sinatra played Juarez."

Now Uncle Tommy Gabriel he still plays Fats Domino.
He speaks that border spanglish well; he owns a carpet store.
He lives out on his pecan farm. "I don't cross the bridge," he says
"'cause everything's gone straight to hell since Sinatra played Juarez."

"Those were truly golden years my, Uncle Tommy says,
"but everything's gone straight to hell since Sinatra played Juarez.
Everything's gone straight to hell since Sinatra played Juarez."

David Lloyd

This Way

*"Will you, for God's sake and for my sake, tell me how you might
be killed? Since my memory is better as a safeguard than yours."
"I will gladly tell," he said.*
        from the Fourth Branch of *The Mabinogion*

It's not easy, Frank told Ava as they lay in bed
after too many drinks loosed his tongue,

even though she never asked,
even though she never cared. Only this way,

Frank explained: Only if when preparing
for my Sunday bath Sammy, Dino, Joey and Peter

follow me in and strip off my tuxedo then lift me
so that one foot rests on the head of a crouching

Bing Crosby and one on the rim of my gold-plated bathtub,
steaming with freshly-drawn water;

and only then if a handsome actor from Spain rushes out
of the bathroom closet waving a knife he has honed

and polished every Sunday for a year,
and only then if that year is the forty-third year

of my life, and only then if the handsome actor
releases my heart from its duties

with three quick stabs and offers it, still-beating,
to the one I love most while Bing nonchalantly

considers the horror above him and my legs quake
and my feet forget their balance and their blood.

Only then, mused Frank, only then will I be truly killed
rather than deeply and endlessly wounded.

All right, said Ava with a bored smile
as she reached for her drink on the night stand.

I'll see what I can do.

Rob Berretta

Frank and Ava's Child

My mother had a wild side, and no one dared to rein her in.
Her appetites were not denied, and this became her greatest sin.
She carried me and wanted love, but stakes were high and life
   was rough.

My father wouldn't dare admit, his pride was strong and
   patience thin,
But soon their love was dry and split, and then he would be
   off again.
It wasn't hard for them to see that nothing good would come of me.

But I was Frank and Ava's child, the fruit of love irreconciled.
I had the looks, I had the voice, but it wasn't me to make the choice.
No it wasn't me to make the choice.

She left Africa for England's shore, a break from shooting in disguise.
Did she leave me there forever more in one last act of compromise?
Or was she so through with Frank by then that this is how
   she thought to win?

I don't know which one declared creation had to be reversed
Or if they would have better fared if I'd have touched their lives
   uncursed.
And what life lay in store for me but second-class celebrity?

But I was Frank and Ava's child, the fruit of love irreconciled.
I had the looks, I had the voice, but it wasn't me to make the choice
No it wasn't me to make the choice.

Beauty is a rarer thing when it comes with stability.
They stand like gods, in praise we sing, but these gifts seldom
   come for free,
And me I carry on a shade, this legend who was never made.

But I was Frank and Ava's child, the fruit of love irreconciled.
I had the looks, I had the voice, but it wasn't me to make the choice.
No it wasn't me to make the choice.

My mother had a wild side.

Suzanne Vega

Frank and Ava

On the way to the bidet
Is when the trouble used to start
It didn't mean she wasn't queen
Of the tinderbox that was his heart

Her fire his desire meant that
Everything must come undone
And so now we know it's not enough to be in love

He's so true she is too she says
I love you Frank and then they drank
All night what a fight
He says it isn't me you're thinking of

She's cool it makes him cruel
And they needle till the jewels
Go raining down upon the ground
She says its not enough to be in love

Not enough to be in love
Not enough to be in love

They woke up and they broke up.
They were volatile and all the while
Life passed it went so fast
And yet they never could forget

Their chemistry like you and me
Proved to keep them both apart for life
And so now we know
That it's not enough to be in love

Not enough to be in love
To be in love
To be in love
To be in love

Daniel Gula

Ava Gardner Said

Ava Gardner Said
check plus in bed   but *trouble*
always was *on the way*
                    to the bidet   What
the hell could ever happen enroute
to a warm water sudsy splash
up "under the hood" bisecting Frank
Sinatra from Queen Bee Gardner   Her ankles
knicked tripping over his hat
again against angles walls make   Or a Tonka
toy a truck left out
But they don't I think have kids
                    cherubs
zonked I am sure if they did on pills and booze and sex or
Betty Ford Center rehabbed
back
Listen   everything's so far away
everything
evaporates any dreams
                    chasing butterflies down through fields
of flowers inside sunshine before the nearby woods
                                wordless & green
below blue hills in the distance   you see
in the distance   everything is
                    beyond us   our capacity
for pain though is present as blades of grass
                                    we trounce
getting there   wherever that may be

Steve Kistulentz

The Sinatra Villanelle

Want to know what was said in that vinyl restaurant booth?
Think Sinatra crying highballs when Ava hightailed it for good,
the mournful croon of I took each word she said as gospel truth.

Order a drink from old Toots: double gin, a splash of vermouth;
light a Pall Mall, eavesdrop from where Gleason stood,
the jukebox whispering what she said in that saloon booth.

She ran off with a teenaged matador, and his bright embroidered suit
hangs on Frank's old oaken hanger, above his polished boots.
That's what you get when you take what she says as gospel truth.

I took out a woman about to leave, dinner as an anniversary truce,
and consoled myself with Manhattans, light on the sweet vermouth,
the night she pronounced our death in a cavernous restaurant booth.

History means mistakes, poking like a child at a loosened tooth,
two stubborn actors rubbing six dollar bourbon into their wounds,
all because they mistook the simplest words we say as gospel truth.

It's last call, but don't go just yet. Be a stand up guy like Frank or Toots
The broad leaves, a pal stays, that's the song. So send a drink if you wou
listen to Frank tell how the story ends, alone in that booth.
I'd always known she'd turn me down. That's the gospel truth.

Blue Tatoo

What Frank Knew

from "My Interview with Orson"

She pauses on the rim
of the sleeping desert,
lights a sweet caporal
with a boot-struck match,
shadowed face floating behind
the arc of a blue diamond

and suddenly she's Ava,
backwoods beauty stolen
from an old movie, playing
a sultry scene in sweat-wet khaki
beneath a California moon,
swaying to forgotten strains

of silent music that tickles
my memory, tighten my senses
and now she turns—
turning to smile at me dark-haired
and dangerous and all at once
I recognize the pull, fall

under the hard draw
of a sucking tide and I am
swallowed, sluiced down a perfect
throat like the perfect shot and
I understand, same as Frank did,
the nature of certain addictions.

Ben Vaughn

Ava Gardner Blues

Standing on a track
Waiting for a train
Holding tears back
But I know it's in vain
No red light coming is gonna ease my worried mind

A love so strong
It put me out
A love gone wrong
Without a doubt
A love with no time for reason or rhyme

Just like Frankie
I can't seem to lose
These Ava Gardner Blues

I could tell by the way she first smiled at me
I knew the day when I'd be free
From the power of her charms
Well, I knew that day might never come

But she cast a spell so hard to shake
I knew so well with every step that I take
That even if I could I would not break these chains and run

Just like Frankie
I can't seem to lose
These Ava Gardner Blues

The way she lied to me
Burns a hole inside of me

So, if there's really a place for broken hearts
Then clear a space and set it apart
For the ones whose owners can't bring themselves to use
Yea, the ones who can't seem to lose these Ava Gardner Blues

Just like Frankie
I can't seem to lose
These Ava Gardner Blues

Leo Luke Marcello

The Swimming Teacher

You gave me that first confidence.
Against my fear of the big cold volume
of water, we overcame by your outstretched
arms and the wriggly wavy lines
of your body beneath the surface.

You were like Ava Gardner to me.
Something stirred inside
I couldn't name.

I wanted to jump,
but didn't know
what would happen
when I crashed through
the cold, blue-green sheet,
the swimming pool surface
in which your warmth waited
and coaxed me to leap.

Don't hesitate, you said.
I leaped, and with every leap
the excitement increased.

And now sometimes when I leap
knowing full well the cold volume,
I still want to take that dare
because I know someone
like you or Ava Gardner
might be waiting.

And even if there's not,
I know, as you have taught,
the water will not let
me drown. So I leap

and look for
outstretched arms,
and I jump.
I jump.
I jump.

Al Alvarez

from Torquil Norman

TORQUIL IS PRESIDENT of the British Toy and Hobby Manufacturers Association, and so a major figure at the London Toy Fair, which takes place at the end of January each year. In 1990, the main story going the rounds of the fair concerned a typical Norman escapade. He had taken a friend for a quick spin in the Cessna to Clacton-on-Sea, on the Essex coast. The Cessna needed an airing, he said, and, more important, Clacton has a fish-and-chip shop where the chips are distinctly superior and the fish comes straight from the sea. He mentioned the jaunt, in passing, to a financial correspondent of *The Times*, who printed the story in the "City Diary,: where it was picked up by the tabloid press and a couple of local radio stations. A number of the bigger players in the toy industry went around the London fair with clippings of the tabloid report and whipped them out of their pockets without provocation, with the sole purpose of embarrassing Torquil.

Partly, it was good clean fun, but it was also a gesture of affection. Quite simply, his colleagues in the trade are proud of him. "Torquil is the British toy industry," said Ken Lewis, a director of Woolworth's. Joe Brewer said, "He's enormously knowledgeable about products, and brilliant at developing ideas. He's also the greatest contact man I know. He knows everybody, and everybody knows him. When someone says 'toys,' everybody thinks of Torquil." Bill Dowle said, "He's a great ambassador for the toy business. He has enriched the world." Even Tom Chamock, who is not given to superlatives, agrees. "You don't have to be very good to be highly regarded in the toy industry," he said. "It's an insular business, sometimes downright incestuous. You have grandfather, father and son all working in the same company. That doesn't really make for innovation. Torquil functions on a different level from the others. He spent a considerable time in merchant banking; he speaks two or three European languages; he has legal training, and his whole educational level is far above the general norm; he is a brilliant sportsman and he flies old airplanes. Back in the Elizabethan days, he'd have been out there sailing the ships, finding us new lands to the west, taking on the Spaniards on the high seas." In other words, the Clacton jaunt was just of those larger-than-life gestures his colleagues routinely expect from Torquil, like a champagne lunch he gave at another fish-and-chip shop the day after Ava Gardner died. He and his friends ate deep-fried cod and drank Moet & Chandon to wish his favorite film star well in the great Hollywood in the sky.

Jarret Keene

Ava Gardner, Queen of Earthquakes

i. The Sinatra Years

Ava, this Sinatra fellow means trouble: his voice is gin,
    but his touch is the devil's testicle, his kiss a gold-
plated revolver. Your white pills are no match
    for the heart-stripping force of a black diamond.
Reconsider his deadly ingredients: a nylon guitar string
    quickens the pulse, candlelight singes the brain,
basil inflames the loins, and wine offers salvation
    only after you absolve it of guilt. Who told you
every antidote is a venom in reverse? But the music!
    My God, his hard-boiled romanticism! The man's
haunted passion and stark irony could wound for hours
    without so much as destroy. Even today there are
men who crank transistors and pretend to be *mafioso*.
    Last we spoke, your gut-shot heart had been left
to spoil, a blown tire on a roadside of dead celebrities,
    their bodies twitching under flash-photography
hailstorms. In between bolts, why not collect
    the blackest pistols? Go ahead: Smuggle one
into your purse and do as follows: Place pillow
    over barrel. Squeeze trigger. Catch feathers.
Hear every blasted note touch your skin.
    Let each object in the bedroom resonate
like an angel's vestment. Listen, Ava. Listen to the toaster.
    Hark, the faux-leopard coat. Trace the radiant arc
of his last swaggering crescendo. Put the vinyl
    to your tongue. Taste the single groove that leads
to the needle, the black spider, Satan. Suck, cauterize
    with fire, bandage, immediately amputate.

There are no victims here, only punishment. A vague,
    terminal power over women. The talent to savage
a beast, to sleep with a torch song that softly cremates.

ii. Ava's Shade Speaks

My face: gored by a young bull,
treated with therapeutic massage,
steam and vapors. The invisible mark
a deathbed curse. In Mexico, there is only
mutilation, the sick dust of make-up.
And to think I'd survived the glint
of a maid's butcher knife. I remember
Hughes's slap dislocating my jaw,
but I didn't fall. Instead,
I fractured his skull with a brass statuette
of his XF-11 photo-reconnaissance plane.
Crack! I cursed him, his impotence,
his Mormon bodyguards.
That night I cooked Southern fried chicken
and mashed potatoes, and let me tell you,
I'm the best gravy maker on this planet.
He chewed slowly; he was no stranger to blood.
He was no swordsman either, but he could eat.

My gallbladder: surgically removed in Spain.
Frank's Catholic bodyguards brought sprays
of orchids. Hemingway touched the incision
like a priest who fears his own death.
"I kill pleasure for animals," he confided.

My uterus: scraped, burned, removed.
I've apologized to all Romeos, those glib
destroyers of sex, who require a radical
inner ugliness to fuel an otherwise bland
outer greatness. My advice? If someone
brings a gun to a knife fight, break his legs.

Place your hands on your lover's face.
Keep them there or he'll seduce other women.

My heart: a prostitute. I married my first husband
at age twenty. But who will save you from fate's
jury-rigged screenplay? Will anyone confess that
the mattress is bullet-riddled? When you're bored,
you take up bullfighting. Sometimes you trap yourself
as a hunter traps an animal. Sometimes you roll
your car over and walk. away. Once,
in a Chicago nightclub, I locked myself in the restroom.
People outside had torn pieces of my black
evening gown for souvenirs. I'd have given them each
a scrap, but my handbag contained a gun,
amphetamines, a matador's phone number, a recipe
for *cordon bleu*. How do you explain these things
to the press, friends and family, the lover
who brushes your cheek with his gifted hands?

iii. Queen of Earthquakes

I even watch your disaster movies: *Earthquake, City on Fire*.
    Secretly, I want the ground to open its train-
wrecking embrace, cars to ricochet against high-rises,
    Charlton Heston to leave you for his sunny mistress.
Yes, I want you to die, Ava, in a Pana-vision of doomsday
    Los Angeles: ripped freeways, shattered glass,
a bridge consuming itself in spasms of stupid pleasure.
    The camera never stops shaking. Where is your face?
Let us rewind this holocaust and pause the apocalypse.
    For nature, unlike history, never fails to remind men
of their errors. In Hollywood, the Richter scale repairs
    misdirected passion, realigns the heart's tortured
landscape. Moreover, during an earthquake, no man
    can leave his woman's side. But here you are
drinking in a flamenco club. Here you are breaking
    George C. Scotts's face with a bottle of cheap
Spanish gin. Here you are dying in a hospital in Rome.

Sinatra's bodyguard nudges you with the Bible;
he mumbles from the Book of Revelations.
    Each word is a sexless cadaver hanging itself.
Indeed, these, your final movies, disaster flicks, are parables
    of glamorous discontent. Confess: you want the world
to collapse upon itself, the lovers to be thrown
    into the blaze. Go on, then, Contessa, dance your way
out of this mess. Here's a time machine: Grabtown,
    North Carolina, 1934: you're fresh-faced again, and
nimble. Your bare feet scamper through tobacco fields
    at twilight. And when the terrain shifts, Ava, as the
earth erupts, someone is holding you, once again, too close.

Lynn Veach Sadler

Ava Gardner Shades the Grave

of Gregory Peck

We were the King and Queen of Beauty,
you and I. Maybe that's why
we could just be friends.
Still, I know
you were too good for me, Old Friend.
I have had no good from men
except your friendship.
Women *and* men liked *you*.

Your earliest childhood was mean and lonely.
Mine was lean and hungry—but crowded.
I never had a child.
Your son committed suicide.
You would have said
it was better to have loved and lost
than to be childless.

I *copied* literature—*movies*, I should say—
expatriated myself to slinky Spain
à la Brett Ashley, but I was no lady
like the Lady Brett.
You?
Before Atticus Finch was, you were.
Lewt McCanles? *Not ever!*
You were the all-time
Poster Boy for Good Guys,
and you a native Californian!

You never thought I was
what my tobacco-barning kin
call a "slut." You knew I had to *play* one.

142

I know it was no cinch to be Finch,
placed as you were.
I was placed where you were.
I *know*.
You managed your Hemingway
without all the masculine stuff
humming like a humming bird in heat.
You were...*solid.*

You told me I was too hard on myself
and other people.
When biographers seized on
my wedding "Mickey Rooney
shortly after joining Metro,"
you said, "Count the '*shortly*'
as magnificent pun,
not puny obsession."
That's the way you dealt with all the hype
of your being such an "*act*-ivist," you said.

Not just Broadway, but *The Stage* loved *you*.
That time you were filming in my home state,
took the flowers to my grave,
you told those state Supreme Court justices
how their daughters should go
if acting careers were what they wanted.
You set out the true *Peck*-ing order:
local theater, then Broadway, then Hollywood.
Did you really do "thirty-some plays
in community theater"?
I know about your helping found
the La Jolla Playhouse.

You got away with being a Democrat!
A "liberal"!
What if you *had* challenged Governor Ronnie?
You *lived* all the causes you fought for.
You were pro-Blacks, anti-Semitism,

made another stand with *Pork Chop Hill*
(which is *still relevant*, I'd say).
Me? Liberal the wrong way, I suppose.
But I'm proud I was friend to Lena Horne,
though she didn't eulogize at my funeral
the way Brock Peters did at yours.
Well, I didn't march with Mr. King,
postpone the Oscars when he was assassinated.
Of all your awards, the Medal of Freedom
suits you best in my opinion.

As we speak, my home state's
having another flap about a book.
The Quran was last year.
This time "they're" "nickeling and diming"
Ms. "Erringright," as you would doubtless deem her.
Does she—anybody—know
you helped Chrysler save
its six hundred thousand jobs?

You were too good for me, Old Friend.
When I came here—
died seems too incisive for *me*—
you took in my Carmen and Morgan.
My leavings: a loyal housekeeper,
a dog as loyal as dogs can be.
You had a "real boy's dog," you told me.
I should have named mine "Gregory."
No, "Eldred," Old Friend.
"Eldred" sounds as Welsh as my Welsh Corgi…
Surely, "Emlyn" is Welch.
Emlyn Williams' *The Morning Star*—
your debut on Broadway.
You've been *morning, noon*…
now *evening* STAR, Old Friend. You were
"The Man for All Seasons." *No act.*
You were too good for me, Old Friend.
That was *no act* either.

144

Lynda Kenney

Ava (a Nod to a Famed Beauty)

Oh, but weren't we beautiful, Stuart.
A girl called Ava was heard to say.
I watched us in a film today
before the drink had had its way
before Frank left me to do it my way.
I was the toast, then, back in the day
I died alone, by the way

Pia Savage

Channeling Ava Gardner

DULCIE WANTED TO LOOK like Ava Gardner. She curled her dark brown hair and plumped her lips out but when she was through looked more like Kate Moss during her drug years.

She patted her concave stomach that was just beginning to protrude. The baby's father looked like Elvis. Surely that gave the baby a chance to look like Ava. Dulcie read everything she could on 50's stars. Walt told her she was obsessed with them.

She didn't like Walt using words like "obsessed." He didn't even have a GED yet was always talking about *On the Road* and other books she was sure he couldn't understand. She couldn't and she had a regular high school diploma and had almost finished beauty school. People said she was good with hair.

Everything had been going so well until Walt's father fell down a hill and was in the hospital for two months. Then they made him go to a nursing home and he died.

Turned out he had never bought the mortgage insurance he told Dulcie and Walt he had bought as a wedding present for them. Damn, they went to the courthouse and got married just because the insurance read Mr and Mrs Wayne Kilgore. The bank accepted the papers Walt's father gave them.

Walt lost his job. Walt was always losing jobs. Now that she and Walt were married he was half responsible for the mortgage but acted as if it were all Dulcie's problem. She didn't know who she hated more, Walt or his dead father.

Walt spent all day on the porch reading books while Dulcie worked six days a week in the town's diner 5:30 AM until Two PM. Soon she wouldn't be able to work in the kitchen anymore. It was already making her feel sick. Three days a week she worked Four PM until closing in the convenience store. Couldn't get more hours. Last time she had been pregnant the doctor made her give up that job. Too much heavy lifting. She lost the baby anyway.

Walt would smoke several joints and drink too many cans of beer. Most of their high school friends had stopped associating with them. Dulcie couldn't blame them. She was friendly with everybody at the diner but no longer had any girlfriends to talk to. Walt wasn't just a mean drunk but a groper.

In between shifts she would go to the library. Today was Thursday; Dulcie could stay until Mrs Whitman closed the library promptly at five. She would get lost in stacks of old movie magazines. Life seemed so simple then. She was sure it wasn't; nothing was simple, but…Ava Gardner didn't have a bank threatening her about a house and beauty school loan. So many men wanted Ava Gardner, including Frank Sinatra–not that Dulcie could understand his appeal. She tried listening to his music and it did nothing. Elvis was much better.

She knew that Mrs Whitman the town librarian didn't approve of Walt, her or her reading material. Dulcie refused to feel awkward. She walked with a grace she was sure Ava Gardner would be proud of. Then she sat and devoured magazine after magazine.

Mrs. Whitman would frown but Dulcie would just smile. Unlike Walt she hadn't stolen books or forgotten to bring them back. Unlike Walt she kept jobs and paid bills, but damn it was hard now. Every cent she made went to one bill or another, and still they owed too much.

Dulcie knew she should ask Mrs Whitman where the books

on bankruptcy were, and for articles on banks taking houses back, but she wanted one more afternoon reading about Ava Gardner.

Clarence Major

Film and Flesh

I was watching a movie
about myself
when I suddenly saw
someone else,
something else—a nightmare figure,
maybe human, maybe not,
maybe the star of a dark carnival—
on the set, entirely realistic,

assume my identity, walking away
with me, explaining nothing
even as he spoke over his shoulder,
saying it's okay; I also play nurses,
matrons, schoolmistresses, doctors.

It's okay? Is it Saturday night and Sunday morning
all the time? Was it okay
with Ava Gardner, in Singapore?

I can sing. I have a brain, muscle and hair,
gastric glands and two eyes. I work
the garden, I am liquid and membrane.
I am not film. I am living, I say.

Allan Gurganus

When I Was Engaged to Ava Gardner

Can sufficient Human Beauty make a farm girl turn to Goddess and her hometown come almost to like itself?

I.

The love of the beauty of the world. . . .involves. . . .the love of all the truly precious things that bad fortune can destroy. The truly precious things are those forming ladders reaching toward the beauty of the world, openings onto it.

Simone Weil, *Waiting for God*

MEN DADDY'S AGE SAVED AVA back till bourbon #3. Even as old guys, they held on to the joy of having seen her. Back when she was sixteen and fresh off a tenant farm over Smithfield way, when she was taking "First Year Secretarial" at Atlantic Christian, back when these pink boys themselves were just eighteen and fairly rich (for Eastern North Carolina), still civilians zipping around in red convertibles right before Pearl Harbor aged them so damn fast.

Of that whole botched last century, maybe 1939 was the best year. That's when she appeared at dances hereabouts.

Their first sight of Ava seemed proof of a perfection fellows drifted back to often. Jack Daniel's helped. Jack and Ava arrived in their lives about the same time; both stayed true friends. Jack's amber can form a little hollow in you, one balanced indentation that reflects the entire sky but is really no bigger than two cupped human hands. As you sit still, talking of things you've loved, something valuable can pool there at your center. You come to guard that like rain collected in a birdbath. Jack made the mirror where Ava's features still showed daily.

The men had just played eighteen strenuous holes. Lifelong pals now collapsed in the red leather clubhouse bar, two guys sat with legs elevated. They kept massaging pulled ham-strings, little pity wasted, barely noticing their lives now tilted past the fulcrum middles. Other buddies, bound home from work, roared in for quick snorts. Me, nine, I was one of their sons. Though my dad was too busy and religious to hang out here, I sat tucked into one corner of the bar (legally not really supposed to be here). Spivey allowed it. He, our most diplomatic and hilarious black barkeep, now whispered, "You gon' keep quiet off at one side, right? We got no choice when this bunch gets telling them same lies, huh?" So, wearing my dry Jantzen suit, waiting for swim practice to start downstairs, I tucked bare legs up under me, settling deeper into leather cushions. Tonight I'd absorb whatever new they might say of her.

(I would one day get to see her for myself, alive, in person, wearing a bathing suit. Preparing for that, dressed in my Cub Scout uniform, I skipped knot-tying class and biked to the Center Theatre. *The Naked Maja*, 1959. Mother warned, "You're not old enough for any Ava movie, especially one with a *naked* in the title." I prayed that the aged lady ticket-taker would let me in. I lowered my voice, rose onto tiptoe, showing extra inches of a uniform that made me look far older. In this way I became the matinee's sole patron, left alone with Ava—feverish, flickerish in white and licorice above me. Her name, immense in the titles, seemed better printed than the rest. Beauty of her proof can almost hurt you as it helps. On the beach, sand sifting out from under your soles feels good before it knocks you backward.

In the middle of her second row, head back, mouth open, I suffered, toying with my scout neckerchief, suckling its ends. Seeing her, I knew the older guys, if anything, had understated. I felt irked: other actors kept walking right into Ava's movie, bothering her. Some scenes didn't even *show*

151

Ava! She packed extra mystery and clout: Ava was somebody who'd started on the horizontal red-clay local but had got so clear of it, so vertical, so fast. Was she a great actress yet? Did I care? With a white gown exposing her whole left shoulder, she tossed her head back, fountaining the most willing mirthful laugh, one almost deeper than the voices of these men here.)

Yes, at last sipping #3, they'd warmed sufficiently toward the Ava topic. Bourbon #1 always involved new business triumphs and old family woes. The Second World War could slosh a guy straight through his second Jack. But the first sip of Drinkie #3 (a not uncommon number for 1959) meant admitting your own brief if deep acquaintance with the very woman who currently electro-charged the cover of every non-automotive magazine sold at Keyser's Drugstore.

And our person did not just look pretty there in print (where someone stayed busy being merely pretty every week). No, she looked Beautiful (big word: like War, Death, titties—one of the biggest). And Ava was beautiful in an unusual, differing way on every one of those slick weeklies: now regal, now "ready," now a tease, now your bratty baby sister, now the Duchess cynical yet tempting in her real pearl choker. But never ever a poor girl off some borrowed broke-down tobacco farm stuck out along the Brogden Road in all-by-itself red-dirt Johnston County. And yet she *was*. That's the miracle of Beauty. Like Grace, like Santa's not knowing rich chimneys from poor, it drops in unbidden. And your ability to pay for an only daughter's orthodontia/dermatology/debut, that's no guarantor of her drop-dead looks, Lord knows. Beauty will just crop up, even on a nowhere tenant farm. It arrives, the silver rebate for generations of ill luck. Seems that Beauty is always looking to get started someplace. Anyplace. And such a spot remains forever after holy. Isn't that what Christmas and the stable and the star is all about?

IF ALL THE CAROLINA MEN WHO SWORE they'd been engaged to our loveliest local had actually offered her a diamond, Ava would've been a major stockholder in DeBeers by the time that child turned twenty.

For you, I can now re-present the testimony of her suitor I knew best. Mr. Wembley's snub-nosed kids held class offices at my school. His daughter Creighton was my favorite partner at the white-gloved children's Ballroom Cotillion; pretty Creighton could take a final slow-dance dip like no one else; she seemed so recklessly sure I would not drop her, I didn't. Those Wembleys always were a pile of fun. Born blond, they'd do anything to keep the party going. All Wembleys got Corvettes at sixteen and, ten months later, had mostly lost their licenses. How can I suggest the sanctity of Wembley cocktail hours? Every room seemed decorated around a different colored marble-topped bar. All locals knew you never phoned a Wembley after 6 p.m. Past then, no message ever got relayed, recalled. Strange out-of-town friends answered the phone, "What?," had no idea who anybody was, kids especially. And didn't that sound like a live jazz combo in the foyer? The Wembleys' youngest son was named Gibson. Why? Because those were mostly what his mom drank that whole long, hot summer she had to be pregnant with him. And Gib's dad was Chalmers Wembley the IV; or maybe V. But let's encourage Chalmers to tell us Ava in his own words, shall we? First go get you a drink. No, three. Then accept all this aloud. And imagine it is springing, baritone, from Mr. Wembley's leather wing chair and footstool so spilled-on it looks to be gator hide. Imagine Spivey, dapper in his white jacket, placing a stiff #3 on the nearby silver tray. Chalmers had mellowed to a graying exec secure in gold-wire specs, his coloring a yachts-man's, hair right thick for a man his age, and vocal tones scented with considerable charm, considerable Jack Daniel's:

"It'd be the April of '39 we drove over to some Azalea Ball at the Greenville Country Club. There were tons of Balls then, every other week. Jackson and Wes and I all wore new white dinner jackets. Those were considered somewhat wild then, mighty citified and 'Artie Shaw,' boys. Passing somebody's silver flask around, we wondered whether stodgy Greenville chaperones would even let us in. But the very second we

153

hopped out of Jackson's red LaSalle convertible, sec we heard the big band going already, when we stepped in as shoulder-to-shoulder white, that dance floor went a little quiet. Especially the girls. Proving we were going to be all right tonight, and maybe a bit more. I saw one big linebacker-looking fellow stare down at his own black jacket. Seemed unhappy with it now. That made me right glad we'd come.

"Greenville was always a fine town for girls. Raleigh, they were snobs. Farmville, they were not but had no reason to be. Perfect balance in Greenville, cooperative. Wearing long dresses, the girls all did look wonderful, being like our ones at home but better for seeming new blood and yet still from families whose names we somewhat recognized.

"I remember the band was a famous one, almost. I'd sent Jackson to the bar for our first drink of many tonight. Heard a new group of kids pile in behind me. Straightening my bow tie, little vain I guess, I checked back over my shoulder. I'd almost blocked the door, so I might just get first crack at whoever good came in.

"Just then—after what I saw—all the girls behind me, the ones that'd just looked mighty copacetic? They had turned bad as chicken salad left outdoors in August. Seemed like I could now recite exactly what was wrong with every last damn one of them. Too much nose, shoulders sloped, red hair overly frizzed, dime-sized freckles, someone powdered to where she looked fallen in the flour barrel. I don't remember the color of the dress the new girl had on. Only that she wore one. Which was too damn bad.

"Because this girl, boys, well, you saw her, some of you fellows. So you know. It was like she had just come in from someplace excellent where she had always been everybody's favorite there. Looked like some Olympic swimmer with her suit on underneath. She seemed that glad to be right in her body. (Who wouldn't? I sure would.) And me, lucky enough to be patrolling this particular double door. Just once in your life you like to fill your eyes clear up with the one that's Perfect.

"You don't know what a big word that is. Not till you see it.

Not unless you're still young and crazed enough to imagine you might get to touch some of it later tonight. It didn't even really make me feel quite 'sexy,' not at first. More like the few times in church when you sense there might really be something, after all.

"She looked so different from the rest of us, this girl could've been a mermaid. Some type of old-timey creature that's human plus....Don't they claim—not to be sacrilegious, Rector Ralph down there—that Jesus was half man, half God? Well, let's call this new girl all woman and half goddess. Now, *goddess* was not a word you heard a whole hell of a lot in poor ol' flat-tire Eastern North Carolina. But it added itself to us that night.

"She made you realize how looking at most other people, even other girls sixteen, it involved, well, a certain amount of eyestrain. You were always squinting, factoring for the aggravation of the bumps in noses, those twelve extra pounds, some hint of a pimple coming or going. Little things you'd silently change if you could, for their sake.

"Around her, there was no such work. (And you wondered: maybe you'd just invented all that other, Trouble, etc., Needing To Die Someday, and so forth?) Excuse me over there, but Spivey? Might I rate a sweetener here and still have this be considered #3? You're a gent-scholar.

"Because to stare at the new girl, you found so little to criticize, it was like your eyes kept sliding off the sides. A face and figure that crackerjack, it somewhat *reorganizes* everything around it.

"The air, the front hall of that none-too-grand Greenville Club. Well, she just stood half smiling, the lidded eyes almost sleepy, maybe to hide her being too alive. She carried a handbag as if trying—comical—to look like other girls. A dark shawl puffed around her, showing off the neck, ideal collarbones, such shoulders. She seemed almost content, just waiting there surrounded by a bunch of other girls come by car from some backwoods county seat. These girls were 'attractive' or just 'striking' but unlucky enough to spend the evening in sight of her and getting constantly compared. Boys, you'll remember our North Carolina motto. 'To Be Rather Than to Seem.' And till this, I mean till *her*, seemed like everybody I'd considered beautiful was only seeming to be. But they'd made that their full-time job. And here she was, just being it so easily. *Beautiful*, most beautiful word. Almost better 'n *rich*, boys. —Thank you, Spivey. And as Spivey will agree, I'm sure, there's few poetry words any sweeter than *rich*.

"But funny, *I* felt I had also just been found wanting, looks-wise. Till recently I was the handsomest boy in here (no offense, over there, my bald old man friend, Jackson). Been feeling fine till she slipped in and messed up everybody's bell curve scale of operations, you might could say. She was a bell curve unto herself okay. I was staring right damn hard I guess. Must have been used to it, that girl.

"So she gives me a kind of bored fish-eye plus one cute smirk. But acted like a grown man laughing, some pool-hall sharpie that's seen it all. I could imagine a tomboy snapping back, 'What are *you* gaping at, you big lug?' It tickled me because us three guys from Falls had just come through that same door like a pack of girlie-girls in brand-new dresses, hoping to make a splash. And here the most beautiful girl in the world had walked through that same door a minute later but had done it like some plain and regular boy would! Not one prissy bone in that whole gorgeous body. A waist I bet I could have fit my big right hand clear around and breasts looking only up up up, respectable, not one ounce of extra weight, just right, what we used to call a perfect mouthful apiece. And here she was, bounced in fresh and about to hum whatever song the band chanced to play next. And *why*—was it possible?—had she been born by accident in driving distance? Of here? Of me?

"I guessed on sight she was a daddy's girl, some county kid with flashy, worthless older brothers she just hero-worshiped. A girl who'd grown up roughhousing with strong buddies and colored kids from down the road, a rounder who could shoot hoops, jump fences, ride the family mule bareback, shimmy down any drainpipe. Black hair with points of auburn in it. Dark green eyes with amber at the centers. They never seemed to blink or bat or keep lowering like our other geisha girls, the way the weak ones did.

"Can't remember how I got the nerve. Stood only three or four steps from her. So I just turned, drew right close, fellows. —Thinking I'd see rouge, but she had nothing on, no makeup. It was all *her*. And it was a face without one pore showing. Plus, it'd sucked all the light out of the ballroom's chandeliers clear here into this darker lobby, then putting even more of it back out, a lantern, I swear. A dividend. By now, my lower-body's stock was splitting, so to speak. The religion, awe, had passed. She had my full-salute attention. I knew the very second any other boy saw her it'd be all over, fellows. Then trombones, synchronized, swinging side to side, started 'When the Red Red Robin Goes...'

"So I go, 'You look like you came here to dance and are really swell at it, dancing. And I'd sure like to learn a thing or three from you.' Or something idiotic. Doesn't matter a bit what stupid thing you say if they like your looks. And, back then of course, I wasn't. . .deformed. Stood at least six-two and healthy. Except, once you'd looked at her, you did feel ...crippled, compared. 'Best offer so far tonight anyways,' she says, all throaty, to her friends with a laugh. They giggled high, but only like girls, whereas she was already a woman with a chest-voice.

"Said, 'Anyways.' Back then only poor kids put the 's' on. That made me even harder. Imagine a Royal going 'anyways.'

"We would dance now. So my hand scooped to the small of her long back, for guiding her onto the floor. Others cleared lots of room, glad to greet us. It was only as I squired her that I felt a trembling. She could not have been cold, it being April. No, poor kid was shaking so from being new here. To this and us. From the thrill of what, to Wes and Jackson and me, was just another so-so Saturday night out. Well, that really got me. I knew then, boys, the main princess at this ball was really Cinderella. A virgin. And you had to touch her to know. And I had. Touched. Her. —So much moxie, that girl. Within a month I'd met her parents. Hard-luck people, nice enough, not bad looking. The mother was already a butterball but with the same skin, and sweet. And her dark father kept real quiet, busy with the constant cigarette. And a few of the sisters had turned out almost pretty, but what'd worked magic in her had only got those others kind of hatchet-faced.

"The family work was babysitting teachers in a boarding house near a school, housekeeping for spinsters. Some fun. They seemed the sort of former tenant farmers who'd had a run of rotten luck you truly didn't want to know about. (Funny, till about thirty-five years later, meaning my last birthday, I'd never once wondered how those poor Gardners saw me that day. Me, speeding up their rutted drive in the convertible Wes leant me. Me, shaking all their hands like a grocer's son running for president of Boys' State. God, our good luck can make such asses of us, can't it? If we're not real careful.) —Spivey, 'nother traveler splash to prolong good ol' #3?

"Within six weeks we were sort of engaged. No ring or anything, but I could see the whole future. I had her rock picked out. She was always so much fun, on top of how she looked, apart from it. She never really counted on that, even later she made these cracks about it. Didn't understand, even as somebody getting really well known, the power of it, you know? The lash of it. We would go into a cafe, and the cooks—black and white—would come out of the kitchen to stare at her, and she didn't seem to notice it was happening. If she said 'hi,' they'd go all bashful but, you know, pleased. I got to see, early on, it was like a burden, carrying around a beauty the Martian scale of hers. Like the way inheriting a huge amount of money takes daily tending to. Somebody's gotta do it. And this was only around here, in Falls. Before Moving Pictures caught sight of it and put their moneymaking mitts on her, spoiling things for purer talent scouts that got there first, boys, right?

"If some date I'd planned didn't quite work out? She was never prissy or fussy like the other girls round here were then. Ava was a sport. Born nowhere with nothing, she blamed nobody, she knew how things got done. I felt sure enough of how I felt, took Ava home to meet Mother.

"Well, you guys remember Mother. Been dead these seven years, but some people still shudder when I mention the ol' battle-ax, God rest her. Since Ava never blinked, never seemed to feel ashamed while meeting a man's stare head-on, she might have been a lot like Mother, come to think of it. We were living in the Big House then, over where Summit meets Monmouth? the old Kenilworth place. And Mother made Zeke come in from the grass-mowing and put on his one dark suit and be the butler for a day, just to scare my poor little date, I swear!

"Ava was wearing a black dress, very simple, and it showed off the skin. She had a brooch shaped like a flying silver bird, swallow maybe. Might've been Woolworth's, but on her it looked like half a mil in platinum, boys. —Spivey, you mind reader, you! Her hair was up, and she stood five-foot-eight-plus in heels, the perfect size. You know, definitely there. The girl had balls, boys. I didn't think I'd like that in a girl, or that she could still be one, with those, but a fellow had to respect knee-knockers that size. Outranked, I reckon.

"Well, she slid into the 'East Parlor,' as Mother made us call it—this poor girl gliding with her head held high just so. And seeing her head-to-toe beauty, I thought Daddy was going to have a stroke. Could hardly get up out of the chair, Dad. I had hinted to him as how she was mighty exceptional-looking, but I'd also said that about four earlier simps and heifers. Mother sniffed at his reaction. But she sure took everything in, grading, judging, a disease with her. Ava acted totally at ease, couldn't have been more natural. Like she hoped to put us at ease here! Momma had felt sure that our white marble hallway and Zeke, with grass-covered work boots showing under his suit, would surely scare off fortune-hunting country girls like this. But Ava, even if scared, she never faked or shied from anything, not even then. If the gal wondered about something, she would flat-out ask. That's how a person learns. Women liked her, even felt sorry at times. But she was a real man's woman, Ava. Which Mother despised, being one herself. Or, no, *wanting* to be. Ava talked about how her people looked after the teachers at a boarding house the county provided over near Wilson. How she'd been taking shorthand and typing courses at the college there, her small plans. Well, Mother was perfectly polite. I guessed her usual rock-solid frost must be cracking here and there with Ava's warmth. I felt glad, proud. Mother finally rose up, said, 'Will you excuse me a moment, Ava? I'd put out a few refreshments in honor of your visit. —Chalmers, could you lend Mother a hand?'

"She pulled shut the parlor's pocket doors. Momma left Ava alone and smiling at Daddy, who slumped there grinning but looking electrocuted. Ava was giving him her 'for-the-daddies' smile. (Fact is, Pop's only true respect for me started and maybe ended that same afternoon.)

"So Mother eases me into the butler's pantry, closes us in. And she says—I remember like it was yestiddy-Mother says, very firmly, 'Well, Chalmers. That is the most beautiful girl I have ever seen in my life. Wears clothes exceptionally well. Very direct and not unintelligent. —But, darling? Trash is trash. It just won't do.'

"So, fellows, you might could say: my loss was Hollywood's gain."

And another man, even further into his #3 than Mr. Wembley—because this other gent had not been jawing through a story they'd all heard three hundred times before— that man saw fit to add, very slowly, like a radio announcer, "No, Chalmers. Not just Hollywood's gain. The *world's.* —'Nother li'l' drink, boys? Just to toast *her*, really."

OVER MY LIFETIME I'VE HEARD NINE MEN TELL versions of this same tale. About their bringing Ava home. About losing her to their own overruling mothers who missed the entire point of that undowried Gardner girl. And I heard at least nine men believe it, every single time. Why? Because she was from here. Because ours was the poorest isolated part of a not-rich state, and so our scale of expectation had drawn way back accordingly. Then she walked in. Because they really had seen her when she was sixteen or seventeen and, because, I swear to God, she was that beautiful. I know.

Elaine Scarry recently wrote, "Our desire for beauty is likely to outlast its object because, as Kant once observed, unlike all other pleasures, the pleasure we take in beauty is inexhaustible. No matter how long beautiful things endure, they cannot out-endure our longing for them."

We usually think of beauty as a brilliant work of art, as the landscape itself, or even some epic act of engineering like putting fellows on the moon. But sometimes it's merely a face. A human face, even a Southern one born at home along a road you know well enough to drive drunk at 3 a.m. Imagine that the favorite of your rustic youth becomes the one recognized by every set of eyes alive as the Most Beautiful Earthling Breathing Right Now. That's something. Keats was right to tie Beauty straight to Truth. I write here of how one person —seemingly chosen by random lottery—became a fact and magnifying lens within the lives of all those living around her, strangers especially. Beauty of this caliber and gradient and force seems capable of changing you forever. Mermaid, saint, something, Lilith, almost monster, it hovers off apart from the rest of us. But always in sight. It is a category of its own, a life-long isolation booth maybe made of clear glass. No place for the seventh in a big, loud county family. Just before her sister took her by train out to Hollywood at age eighteen, contract in hand, the poor girl, almost embarrassingly tapered and ideal, sat in the loaner LaSalle alongside young Chalmers. And Ava shook her head, "People carry on sometimes. I know I don't look real bad. But, hell, baby, I can't *see* it."

Poor her. She was the only one.

Decades after she'd got famous in a way whose improbability we alone on earth could really appreciate, she was down here visiting the Chalmers Wembleys. He'd married a brunette named Eva that some folks called "an Ava look-alike," but everybody knew that there was no such thing. And it was beside a neighbor's pool that Chalmers had borrowed so she could swim without being hectored by what we then called "autograph hounds" that I saw her myself. I've got to tell you about that later. My time. With Ava.

We all lived on a first-name basis with her: it wasn't really meant disrespectfully. No other white girl we knew was ever called Ava. And unlike most of us in the owning classes—a small group where your last name always told the most about you—she hailed from beholden renters out of Grabtown beyond Brogden past even Smithfield. She'd sprung from nobody who owned anything that'd even be worth carrying to your car. And so, we—entitled ourselves—just claimed her and took credit, sort of, as if we had, all along, been her broth-ers, sons, lovers, all the above. We lived in tobacco fields the Railroad only crossed with tracks to get folks elsewhere fast. (Incest? Anybody from Eastern North Carolina having sex with anybody from Eastern North Carolina, it's already incest. —So why hold back with *her*?) But imposing and refined as she could look, so ladylike, it was only "like." We knew what was underneath or hoped we did. What I mean, of course: we all really, really wanted to jump her. You knew it'd be beyond satin, very wet, and getting loud right fast. You wanted it not just so you could say you had. No, better to do that secretly and then have it between just the two of you. That'd mean you had just saved your own life. Thanks to the goddess, you'd gone God. Everything after would be bonus.—So, hey:

Let the Swedes claim Garbo.

Let the Krauts keep Dietrich.

But this one? She was born a Princess left, by accident, in the care of woodcutters, Gardners.

And since we were the only Princes hereabouts in this most sad, level, farmed-out sector of our state—since we were, after all, its males, its heirs and owners, we made her simply "Ava." Simply ours.

II.

Pretty is as pretty does.

Old wives' tale

IF DADDY'S AND CHALMERS'S CROWD over-estimated Pleasure, it was because their poppas long ago had worshiped Property. Men my grandad's age paid for the red convertibles and white dinner jackets of their romantic, alcoholic sons. They financed such deco-extras, how? By owning dirt farms. They still ran these by the rules of 1870. You used sharecroppers to work your acreage. And such tenants, the son of dispossessed people that Ava's were, it was they who really paid for your boy's smooth silver cigarette case, his black satin collars jagged as bat wings. Odd, I usually felt most at ease with geezers Grand's age; I learned more from their hard-boiled facts than off those wistful, silvering boy-men like our professionally charming Chalmers Wembleys.

(How many sons of owners have imagined the tenant farmer's daughter, growing up on land you know is really yours? How many such lucky boys picture "a warm afternoon at the edge of the cotton fields, her washing clothes by hand in your clear stream, her stripped to the waist and gleaming in late light, and the young man of the place, astride a white horse, out checking the fences, comes across her—stripped, defiant, and yet fumbling to cover herself—as he dismounts. She turns, shy yet wanting, knowing, not unwilling, guessing her true worth...." And that girl was always either Lena Horne or Ava Gardner.)

I loved riding out in Grand's old-timey black Packard, ready to survey all he owned, all that others worked, all I foolishly figured I would one day count as mine. The unsurpriseable men of Grandad's generation looked flinty, hobnailed, ridged; they seemed more mineral than animal. Their watches, like pets, they kept on chains; gold chains, but chains. These fellows hailed from a time when women were either real ladies or really not. A time when your need to know the exact hour was never so unseemly in its rush that you couldn't leisurely coax its chain and open its case like a clamshell and see what property you had to ride over and check on next. No hurry. They were boss men. And they owned families like the Gardners.

Grandad told me he had two kinds of white tenants: The Shiftless and the Luckless. And though the Shiftless were heartbreaking and long-sitting, they were better than your earnest Luckless any day. "See, son, you can send the Shiftless packing between crops. They'll at least leave your barns behind intact. Too damn lazy to steal anything very heavy. But the Luckless! You know what follows them from place to place? It'll turn up a year or so after they do and ruin you all. —Fire, son. Fear the Luckless. They will burn your ass flat down. And they won't blame themselves or even that stray spark. No, they'll blame you, son. They'll blame luck. —See, that's what keeps' em Luckless."

My grandad knew the man whose farm the Gardners burned.

YES, AVA GARDNER ARRIVED on Christmas Eve, 1922 into that very overheated line. I mean the most stigmatized branch of a tribe called Luckless. The Fire-prone.

Later, men would praise her speaking voice as "smoky;" her body, they claimed, had "the kick of dynamite"; her singing voice held the singe of a "born torch singer." Newspapers didn't call the girl a bombshell for nothing. Long tradition, that.

Jonas and Molly Gardner, pre-Ava, were certifiably Luckless. Then the Depression came. Along with drought and croup and Hoover, an unplanned seventh baby. Mrs. Gardner was onto forty, her husband forty-four; they'd believed themselves to be too old to conceive yet another mouth to feed. The Gardners had already been turned off the last farm they'd agreed to cultivate for a piss-poor percentage.

When one sort of people gets very tired, they expect to break a little inherited porcelain. With others, spontaneous combustion. And what the Gardners burned always seemed borrowed.—Jonas living by the grace of his landowner in a house on loan, used dynamite to clear bottom land, remove stumps. This was back when the main job of America seemed to be knocking down all those nuisance trees left in the way when Columbus turned up. (A battle yet continuing.)

Well before Ava's birth, a neighbor came to borrow dynamite the way city folks might ask for sugar. And one brass explosive cap fell free. Molly, ever orderly, swept that with other litter into the fireplace. Little Raymond, the two-year-old son, was playing before the hearth. The Gardners' whole chimney went off. And, like a javelin, one length of sharp burning log fired through the room—direct into the child's viscera, impaling him. Though the parents rushed him to a doctor in Smithfield eight jostling buggy-miles away, he didn't live out the next day, poor chap. Accidents happen. So do jinxes. Raymond's gravestone, a life-sized baby angel, shows that the Gardners overpaid, shelling out a couple quarters a month forever, torn up with the guilt.

But such ill luck—it's no one's fault, is it? Then brother Jack (future state legislator, thanks to his jawline and Sister's future renown) came of smoking age. Though Jack—real name "Jonas Melvin"—was living on this farm that grew tobacco, though he was the son of a dad who chain-smoked and would later pay dearly for it, the Gardners were still God-fearing folks: therefore a boy of thirteen had to sneak a cig. So, needing to light up, Jack stepped—not into the woods—but inside a tobacco barn beside a cotton-curing house, the air of both as full of fiber as your down quilt is. And when he struck that match, the barn blew up, taking hair off his head and blunting his thick eyelashes, leveling the landlord's cotton gin and half a farm's outbuildings. One of Baby Ava's first memories: being held up before a window to see the entire tenant farm on fire. It had recently been someone else's. The Gardners needed a new position.

Since they were white and self-respecting if demonstrably Luckless—their community offered them a last crack at dignity. Molly Baker Gardner was one of nineteen children. She'd had to mother herself and many others, usually at the kitchen stove. Now, famous for her baked goods, Molly found herself feeding eight spinster teachers in a boarding

165

house twelve steps from the school next door; Mr. Gardner did odd jobs, serving as handyman at the Teacherage, as it was charmingly called. I have set foot inside this place. I visited decades later. By then it'd become the first and most evocative site of the Ava Gardner Museum. This white-frame structure was windy, cobbled-onto, rough yet affable. You could imagine its front parlor on some autumn Sunday, filled with myopic rocking-chaired teachers all crocheting shawls. You could just hear the seven shoeless Gardner kids lunging in and out "Close that door! If I've told you all once..." There would be the smell of cooling sweet-potato pies, and one spinet kept busy all the Sabbath with thumping hymns in 3/4 time. For her whole professional life, Ava Gardner would be described by New Yorkers, Californians, Europeans, and Press Agents as a hick or a hillbilly. In fact, her parents had been landowners who'd lost everything but ownership's precious memory. As for "hillbilly," Johnston County's topography lies as flat as a good table. There are no hills around for anybody to be billy of.

But what the girl had, her great funding source, the only real luck possible among the countless children of the Luck-less: She sprang from a family that adored its every member, certainly its baby, the prettiest ever. If the South's fierce loyalty to its own is of times judged a failing, there is a beauty in it, too.

Downtown on Market Day sidewalks, foot-traffic clogged with folks lining up to look in Ava's wicker baby carriage. Pride of place can make the State Fair's blue-ribbon 800 lb. pumpkin an entire county's moral triumph. Naturally everybody felt enlarged that such ideal features had accreted here. It was downright Agricultural, a feat like this. For once, the Freakish—let loose among the Luckless—worked our way!

IN TIME, HER HANDSOME BROTHER JACK would pay for Ava's year at secretarial college; her savvy older sister would arrange to have a record cut of Ava's singing. When that went nowhere, this same stalwart sister Beatrice, known as Bappie, would get a photograph of their family beauty into the window of her hubby's photo studio in far New York. Ava was discovered not because some Manhattan producer in a Miami-bound limo chanced to see the goddess Diana astride a passing mule. No, Ava Gardner is known to us thanks to the tender, continuous faith of her own not-rich people. Betterment. Whatever filament of string they had to pull, they yanked with all their might. And, once her stardom lit the sky over the little town of Smithfield, nobody enjoyed Ava's visibility more than they. Membership at last. Soon the Gardner family crest, five feet high (generic, from a catalog), distinguished the front wall of brother Jack's new restaurant downtown. In the end, maybe her siblings enjoyed Fame more than Ava herself did.

Her mom was one of those white ladies peculiar to the working South; I mean the kind that gains large amounts of weight in their upper arms. First a pleasant quilting all over; soon a vaccination scar grown two inches deep. Ava's sisters took after Mom. And who else but Ava Gardner would put their pictures in her autobiography? There they are, gathered at a Smithfield dining-room table, Ava looking ponyish and darling in a man's white shirt. Her grinning sisters wear their best church suits (which make a fashion mistake, revealing upper arms). The married sisters are named (and not by Flannery O'Connor) Inez Grimes and Elsie Mae Creech. Yes. And they sit smiling hard at Ava, and all three have come to eat.

It should not surprise you to know she's buried right with them out at not-pretty Sunset Memorial Park on U.S. 70, resting there faceup among her siblings in a grave not one jot different from their own.

Locals still love Ava because she never did quit loving—if not us—then *here*. Ava came home as often as she could. No surprise she had the locally famous barbeque, still warm, jetted to her worldwide. She served it to fancy friends as a delicacy, always a little better with French champagne. Who would've blamed her for being one of those gals who—passing as classy—gets out and never once looks back? Instead, all her very visible life, she could be counted on to entertain visiting wall-eyed third cousins and not-riveting ladies' book groups come North from Eastern N.C. She'd rent tuxedos for the cousins and take them right to 21. The gal had balls. And she always had sufficient chic so anybody she liked—everything she ever thought was fun—got mighty doggone chic then, too.

III.
Beauty prompts a copy of itself....The generation is unceasing. Beauty, as both Plato's Symposium and everyday life confirm, prompts the begetting of children: when the eye sees someone beautiful, the whole body wants to reproduce the person.
Elaine Scarry in *On Beauty and Being Just*

WOMEN MY MOTHER'S AGE KNEW ALL OF AVA'S movies and saw them more than once in groups of three or five. These ladies lived within twelve blocks of each other; they would pop in unannounced, offering welcome intermissions and the chance for a quick drink before five. It was also considered polite to bring along your latest bit of idle Ava lore.

Such sophisticated women would never have subscribed to *Photoplay* or *Modern Screen*. Nor would they ever patronize a beauty shop that didn't. —They could tell you the year and month when each of that poor Gardner girl's three marriages ended. Or, to use film magazines' diction, "shattered" or "foundered on the jagged rocks below where so many Hollywood unions die violent deaths in that sunny zone of competitive beauty, dubious morals, and, yes, torrid daily temptation."

Unlike their lawyer husbands, these ladies seemed to understand the backlot politics of moviemaking. "Oh, that's not a real romance. The studio just made Ava go to that opening with Rory because he's new out yonder, needs to be seen." Husbands tended to think of Ava's amazing looks as a kind of cow-catcher commodity, something she might wield, track-clearing. True, men Dad's age publicly gathered to discuss how they themselves had seen Ava young, four whole times, and at whose house, and how they'd danced one waltz (and danced it very well if they did say so). Yes, they went on to admit they could have maybe "had" her, if they'd done seven little things a little different. But how many of her films had they really seen? "*Show Boat*, wasn't she in that? Exceptional motion picture, excellent color." Knowing more, ladies lowered their voices whenever her melodic first name arose.

Neighborhood wives and moms, visiting our house, were soon seated on sectional sofas, sipping Manhattan #2 (or, in summer, Tom Collins, same number). They were not interested in sports, in having "scored" off Ava. They seemed readiest to cozy up against the friction, the complex emotional needs of this all-too-visible-oh-so-familiar woman. Half in honor of their subject, who still hated wearing "hard shoes," ladies kicked off their flats. Their hubbies would say most anything anywhere, but female klatches and covens convened "in the home." Amid modern decorator throw-pillows but still in sight of Great-Granny Templer's silver tea service, it felt safer here. Whatever mischief a famously impulsive wife of Falls' fourth best dentist got into with some young bag boy at the Express Line of the Piggly Wiggly, Ava could usually outdo her. For one thing, Ava was an artist. She might be an earthy artist, but that ideal earth of hers was good, rust-red, high-iron-content Carolina stuff, which put us all close to cousinhood.

For wives and moms who felt overburdened, kept down, Ava's recent ascent was like having a U.S. president who'd been in third grade with you. Only better. Presidents' movies didn't play one whole month a year at the Center or the Cameo, or even, across town, at the Booker T. I liked staying home during meetings of the ladies' film-discussion group. Despite their tempting bowls of almonds or pretzels, I never sat in the room with Mom's friends. Huddled amid their rumors and cigarette smoke, I would have felt a bit ashamed. Unlike men at the Club who loved an audience of Young Turks, these women's candor, their low-down wit, always seemed impeded by the presence of a male. Even a nine-year-old. Whatever man came in sight, they deferred to him, just couldn't help it. So exactly as I watched Ava in awed silence from the second row, I eavesdropped on the bawdy wit of local ladies who believed they'd finally been left all to themselves.

They enjoyed a great source for red-meat Ava news: Two Smithfield beauticians worked (very hard) on Ava's heavyset stay-at-home sisters. And since the owner of Falls' best salon spoke with those loose-lipped hair-burners daily, his gossip proved high-grade, recent as a hangover, accurate to the penny. Mom's pals hinted what Ava earned per picture and how unfair that was, considering all MGM made off her talent and looks, not necessarily in that order. The studio grossed a million dollars when they lent her out for *The Barefoot Contessa*. Ava's take? Sixty thousand before taxes. Heck, even Farmer Gardner, sharecropping, anonymous, got a percent-age far better than his famous girl's. Who was our glamorous Ava? Dripping in ermine and borrowed emeralds, hell, Ava was still Labor!

Guys at the Club seemed to think she owned the cameras, booked the theaters. They overrated both her fortune and con-trol. The favor they paid a woman more famous than they? Making her one of the boys, promoting her to Management. And shuttle-diplomat over-hearer that I was, I soon under-stood something major: men are really far more romantic than women. Isn't that true? We men live all or nothing; war's a specialty. Big game. We care most about what's ours, what we saw once, whatever we can say we really own or might. My math teacher praised boys as abstract thinkers, girls were merely literal, domestic, only Realists. But Ava somehow reversed that. I remember hearing Chalmers praising Ava's balls, her going after everything that he himself, neutered by luck and manhood, had simply inherited, the fourth (or fifth?) in line for it.

Women sounded more practical because they were more emotionally precise. They knew what they could bear, which was far more than they ever dared admit. And whenever they saw Ava go after some man or role she liked, they felt assuaged, as glad for her as they were comforted *they* need not risk all that in public. That she had started here and gone so far, it held them in such loyalty to her. It also made the outer world seem less cold. And yet their pity was a part of her importance to them. These funny, talkative women had somehow learned to live with compromise, to accept their laugh lines. A certain margin of loss you just expected. Even as Ava Gardner did. She'd never once considered facial surgery. "Won't go back up. Good while it lasted. This is it, babe."

Strange, but war veterans Chalmers's age seemed more dreamy and fragile, more naive. Neighbor ladies were surely the sharpest critics of Ava's films. The pasty-faced bachelor who reviewed for our local paper knew nothing compared with Mom's cinema coffee klatch. They could tell you which recent movies "wasted" her, and which "let you see who Ava really is." True, they'd only known her in some small social way from the old days. She was not a girl who—if merely mortal, only ordinary looking—they would have ever laid eyes on except downtown during Saturday Market Days when farm kids gathered to make out behind the statues near the court-house. Still, having seen her twice at parties, ladies felt free to say which roles were most like her.

They mourned Ava's Southern accent: some sinister coach at MGM had squashed it before that child got quite unpacked. The one time she performed a script by Tennessee Williams, ladies praised Ava's joy in his language so lyrical and imaginative that only a fellow Southerner could truly sing it. They railed against Elizabeth Taylor's getting to star in *Cat on a Hot Tin Roof*. True, Liz looked right shipshape in that pointy slip. But her voice had stayed that of the prettiest child star ever. Liz's baby-doll whine was so nasal it undid most of her earnest acting. Imagine instead the naturally throaty Ava as Maggie. She was born to play that smart girl from the wrong side of town, married into its richest family, someone put there only by her looks while that poor girl's spirit, her wild and healing spirit, went overlooked. What a waste! Why, she was Maggie the Cat.

171

They liked Ava best as the slightly shopworn, bighearted woman, someone who'd slept around but had not yet found it. Mom's friends thought Ava best when she let loose. *The Night of the Iguana* or *Bhowani Junction* really gave her some emotional heavy-lifting. She moved like a dancer or an athlete or, no, like an excellent farmer's most diligent and happy daughter. Mom hated seeing Ava just standing around wearing the clothes and hairdo. And as Ava complained to her sisters all the time, she would ask a director about her character's motivation, and even her supposed pal John Huston replied, "Don't worry, sweetheart. Just stand there and look beautiful. That's all you have to do."

Mom's pals boycotted Bogart. He was from an upper-middle-class family and had gone to Trinity Prep, but did that give him the right to humiliate Ava like that on the set of *Contessa*? Did it? He called her "the Grabtown Gypsy." Drunk as usual, he hollered to the director in front of everyone, "Hey, Mankiewicz, can you tell this dame to speak up? I can't hear a goddamn word she says." (It will not do, Humphrey, not in North Carolina. Word travels, you alkie lout, you.)

Iguana was shot in a hard-to-reach Mexican coastal village, and Ava, staying in a bigger resort, water-skied to work each day. She'd intentionally worn no bra or panties to get into character as Maxine. Finally she could use her Southern accent in a film. *Iguana* was shot in sequence, not out of order as their usual way of saving money on the setups. And Mother said, "You know, I think Huston did that just to help her give the great performance he knew was in Ava. And it's funny, but even her accent gets better as the movie rolls on. As if she had forgotten how to sound 'from around here.' But by the end, after saying 'honey' enough, she'd regained all that and more. "

Her best scene is where she offers her entire hotel and livelihood to Deborah Kerr and Richard Burton because she thinks he loves Deborah and not her. "Ava acts enraged. But you can see how her respect for love itself, her love for him is just so huge she'll give everything away. That's one of the best things she's ever done," Mom shook her head. "Right then you saw clear into her huge heart. Like these new ranges with the glass doors to keep track of what's burning."

SO I ALWAYS SAT IN THE DEN, ONE ROOM AWAY, attending to their lilting voices. The sound offered a strange mix of shrewdness, affection, and pity. I didn't understand the pity. Not till later. Foolishly, too maley, I thought this meant gals were just being catty: housewives' revenge on a great star. But her bad reviews infuriated my mom and her pals. "In *On the Beach, Newsweek* says, 'Miss Gardner has never been better or looked worse.' —Can you imagine reading that about yourself?" Mother asked. "First they tell her she's too beautiful to live, then when she finally does something solid and true like that, they complain she's not beautiful enough anymore to bring it off. I could wring the critics' necks for her. Someday they'll claim they always knew how good she really was, you watch." Mom's crowd understood that if Ava had stayed home, if she had married Chalmers Wembley IV or one of her other swains, she might've been, like some of them, pretty darn not-unhappy.

I could sure picture her taking tennis lessons and making casseroles, bringing up a bunch of fearless kids that would definitely send a little substance and fun back into our thinning local bloodstream. And local women knew—unlike their husbands—that Ava was not getting whatever else on earth she wanted. She chose the men who rightly saw her as the ultimate treasure and score, but things always went wrong. Even in Hollywood she seemed to want a sort of Johnston County marriage. One where she'd stay barefoot in capri pants beside the stove. But she had her own career, too. She was so jealous of her men and finally so unsure as a girl who'd gone from being dirt-poor and overlooked to well-off and constantly observed. No training in between. Only her parents' decent marriage and the low-end Johnston County Public Schools to be her teachers, the luckless child.

ONCE WE WERE WATCHING Elvis Presley on TV, and my mother said, "I feel so sorry for that boy. He's had no

173

preparation."

I snapped, "For what? He's just the most famous doggone person in the world."

"He's nineteen years old, and his parents have never had two nickels to rub together, and he has no friends he can trust that aren't on payroll. That's got to be the loneliest position. You cannot win from there. "

She seemed to imply that having middle-class fork knowledge and book understanding and good advisors you needn't hire but who would always tip you in the right direction, that was the luckiest thing in the world. Now, I see she was right. And, for Ava Gardner, imagine the benefits of four years at a good college before MGM became her alma mater. What might those have done for her confidence, the roles she chose? (Just one Oscar nomination, but she's far better than anyone ever admitted; better than she ever quite believed.) But this is idle speculation. Everybody knows that girls from her part of the countryside, they never went to a real college. One full year at secretarial school, that in itself showed a blind ambition back then and there, for them.

Even as she aged past first popularity, Mother and her pals "kept up." They felt her battling to make a living but also wanting to leave some beautiful work. They knew all about her ruinous insecurities. How Greg Peck told her she needed to do some live theater at the Pasadena Playhouse, and even got the studio to agree to that, but she was too nervous to take leading parts! Poor thing, willing to make bad movies in front of millions but too scared to risk learning her trade before two hundred. MGM said no, they could not let a major talent be reviewed in the role of a maid and ingénue. Then she railed against how repressive the "owners" were, how they exploited her. And yet she lacked the nerve to really press out on her own.

My grandfather used to accuse his tenant farmers, thirty miles from that farm the Gardners burned, of being "mainly professional sitters. Even the baby ones hate to crawl far." While she was making *The Barefoot Contessa*, Ava agreed to wait on a couch till the cameraman got his lens setting right. Her director happened to walk past and, not knowing why she was so patiently stationary, he snapped, "You are the sittin'est goddamn actress I've ever worked with." For once, Ava, usually salty with words learned from her older brothers, just sat on, speechless. No doubt remembering childhood accusations from owners like my grandad. She was modestly human in a profession that requires monster-vanity. How could the most famous face on earth be self-effacing? It worked for her with the tech crew and her housekeeper and her nieces. But otherwise it went against her. Once, she saw Bette Davis in a hotel lobby. Ava, forgetting her own revised station in life, rushed up like any bumpkin, blurting, "Miss Davis, I'm Ava Gardner, and I'm your biggest fan." And Bette's reply? "Of course you are, my dear. Of course you are." Ava was not the least insulted. She loved that. She had not expected to be recognized; she would never have believed a compliment, returned. "Now that's a star," she said, heartily approving the playful put-down of herself.

MOM AND HER CO-CONSPIRATORS had ever fewer illusions about Ava's three husbands than they did their own. They understood all Ava Lavinia Gardner's luckless choices and what each worthless man had cost her. Was that not her real tradition? Unluck, even now. The tradition of a big guy who gets drunk and belts you one every so often, beats you like a good rug made more valuable. —Did stardom counteract that? The constant ruination by unsolicited fire? Didn't fire always turn up a year or so later, explosions, the divorce? Mom, like Chalmers, retold Ava till the star's very unlikeliness started to make sense:

"Who even knows what she saw in that braying little burro Mickey Rooney? Well, but remember he was # 1 box office then. Earned more the year of *Gone with the Wind* than even Gable did. Ava hadn't been in California six months when Mickey spotted her on the soundstage. And him wearing a Carmen Miranda getup for the movie musical with Garland. Imagine being secure enough to walk over to the likes of her while he wore the tutti-frutti headdress and a coconut bra and still trying to pick her up, right in front of her chaperone sister, dear Bappie. Everybody knows she was a virgin when she married Mickey. And how did he spend most of his honeymoon? Playing golf with his buddies, three guys he put up right in the hotel to have a morning foursome, then flirting with a hatcheck girl. And while Ava waited, lonely, in a sheer white nightie upstairs. The pain. (Unforgivable, Mickey! What is *wrong* with you?) Those two only stuck it out one year and a week. But I'm sure that little show-off was an absolute monkey in you know where....

"As for #2 Artie Shaw, well he was certainly an eyeful then, self-taught and smart but cold all the way through. He sent her to an analyst, made her read Thomas Mann and take college courses because she embarrassed him at parties. He called her a hillbilly and hated to see her barefoot. And he dropped her so she'd hear about it on the radio before he even told her, the poor kid. Crushed. No wonder she had so little self-esteem despite looking like that. Coming from those people, she seemed to attract these continental jerks no better than rednecks from the old days.

"Frank, of course, was the one meant for her. Number 3's the charm. Sinatra had come up hard, and so had she, and they were loyal to their families (except, I guess, when he dropped his wife and three kids to marry Ava). They were both night people. She never really felt alive till very late, and, of course, in Las Vegas, half the population never sees the desert daylight. And they both had all this firepower in the erotic part of things. But there's your trouble, they were like flames meeting flames with nothing left to burn. She told her sister Inez that, with Francis (as she alone got to call him), when Ava couldn't get through to him by phone, round the clock any time of the night she wanted him, she always considered killing herself. Not him, mind you.

"They were both so possessive that, if they stepped into some nightclub, and if a man then looked at her or a woman looked at him—and who *else* were people going to stare at?—their jealousy just mangled each other. She campaigned to get him the role in *From Here to Eternity*, the one that restarted his career and won him an Oscar. And he thanked her by staging his own suicide while she pounded on a hotel door, fired shots into the mattress, and her rushing in and him nude in bed facedown then rolling over, 'Hiya, Ava.' They weren't, well, mature. Even a little. One or the other had to be, at times. Instead they set each other off. So did Romeo and Juliet, and look how they wound up. —But, why she aborted Frank's child, who'll ever know. Spite? Her paying him back after some scene? But I bet you any amount of money that's what she will spend her waning years wishing most to change. What a wonderful mother she would be, Ava. Heck, she called everybody 'baby' anyway, bullfighters, even bulls probably. And imagine that child of Frank's and hers, especially if he was born a boy and what he might have looked like, and, considering the sexual umph between those two, the joy he might have given half the world by now! The miracle is—with all the pistols Frank's goons had on hand—those two didn't literally kill each other. Just for the fun of making up later! It had to end. It never really ended. She wouldn't take a cent of alimony from him. That's the last great way to a man's heart.

"But you want to hear the best record he ever made (or most anybody else)? Try the one he cut just after forfeiting that baby plus her. You listen to *In the Wee Small Hours*, you'll know what all she must have meant to Frank. Put that on around three in the morning, you'll be sure he understood exactly what he'd lost, and right away. It starts with 'Glad to Be Unhappy,' goes to 'Can't We Still Be Friends?,' swears 'I'll Be Around,' then finally claims her as 'This Love of Mine.' Nobody ever put more of himself into songs that he didn't write. It's like he's inventing them a verse at a time at the darkest hour of the morning. And if you listen to it enough, the strangest thing is, you forget about him and what a wizard he is at putting the lines across. You just take for granted the perfect Nelson Riddle arrangements that people are still copying. What you're left with is this complete picture of her, in that slinky black dress she wore in *The Killers* as Kitty. You'll know what amazing company she was, how lively and funny and raw but good. His singing takes you so far into the pain of losing somebody who's that grand a person, plus beautiful in a way not often seen on earth before, and crazy passionate as well. By the end, it's almost like her leaving just happened to *you*. Go buy another copy of the album. I'm always lending out mine, and people never give it back. Seems they think, as with Ava, the one they have is the only copy of it ever made.

"Let's just thank God she didn't marry that next nasty little sadist, George C. Scott. He came later, of course. When her drinking between jobs had puffed her up like cortisone. He beat her so, broke her arm, pulled half the hair out of her head. But she kept going back, mad about him till the worst thrashing, till he threw their whole film off schedule while everybody waited for her to recover. And those two were making *The Bible*! Him Abraham to her Sarah. His whipping Ava put the production back so many days that, on the set, even the technical guys would turn away when he walked in. Just turn their backs on him. Shameful. Finally Frank sicced some of his thugs on Scott to sort of get his attention, make him leave her alone.

"Oh, she's made the choices everybody else in her position would, I guess. But some absolute lulus, huh? And to wind up so totally alone after all of that. You wonder if she wonders about not marrying one of our boys, sparing herself so much? At least she wouldn't be stuck retired in London, a place she chose so she'd not be followed and pawed on the street. They do leave her alone over there, but isn't that a problem, finally? Where did it get her, all of it? Spend an evening with her, she's the most fun in the world. Such an enjoyer. It's all right now. No pretense, never a la-di-da. But you know it's hard, being somebody who always disappoints because she used to look a certain way. A way that everybody needed so they'd feel better about themselves for about a decade and a half. I can imagine being Ava at the top. But now she lives with a nice black housekeeper-companion and two corgis and her cigarettes and the cocktails and whatever offer comes in from *Knots Landing*, I don't know. What must it feel like, being Ava now?"

"Oh, well," someone finally said. And, sun setting, the young wives and mothers sighed, snuffing out their lipsticked Salems, taking a last pull off their tall, dinky glasses, they slid back into their flats and stood, "A woman's work is never done. Got four hungry male animals of all ages waiting to be fed next door, girls." And laughing, they left, half rejuvenated. —Not Ava, more than half glad now.

IV.

I came into this world at ten o'clock at night, and I've often thought that was the reason I turned into such a nocturnal creature. When the sun sets, honey, I feel more, oh, alert. More alive. By midnight, I feel fantastic. Even when I was a little girl, my father would shake his head and say, "Let's just hope you get a job where you work nights." Little did he know what was in store for me. It takes talent to live at night, and that was the one ability I never doubted I had.

Ava Gardner, *Ava: My Story*

DID I TELL YOU I MET HER ONCE?

At school, Creighton Wembley sputtered their family secret. I vowed not to tell one soul: the very next Saturday, Ava Gardner would be staying one night only at the Wembleys. Ava and Chalmers had kept up their fitful jokey correspondence. If she sent him a jar of caviar, he mailed back a box of grits, etc. Whenever he visited California on business, he phoned; they laughed about the bad old good ol' days. Since the Wembleys' swimming pool was late being finished (despite the contractor's specific Ava-ready promise), they had borrowed the pool-equipped patio of a family just down the street. The Kincheloes had been bribed: keys to the Wembley beach house. This cleared the coast for Ava, between pictures and determined to relax with her shoes off. Creighton whispered, "I would ask you over to meet her and all. I remember that you like her. But, see, Daddy said absolutely no gawkers. Not that you *would* gawk." Right.

I rose very early that Saturday. With some care, I chose the bathing suit most flattering, one that might put some age on me. The party would surely not commence till the sun reached its full tanning power. That gave me four full hours to prepare to be invited.

In front of the Wembleys' mock-Tudor pile, long black cars with New York plates sat lined as for a funeral. Two houses down, capping a street corner all its own, the Kincheloes' pool. It claimed a little hill above car level. Topaz blue could only be glimpsed between slats of a high white Williamsburgy fence. From the street you never saw more than an occasional splash to prove how cool it must be on the hilltop. And she had spent the night in Falls, N.C. We'd inhaled the same night air!

I owned a trusty green Schwinn. Indulging a recent fad, I'd clothespinned playing cards (two queens) against my bike's front axle. Moving spokes stuttered cards into a motorized putter I considered neat. I felt that any engine noises not made by mouth leant me age, style, gravitas.

By 9 a.m., trying to act casual in swim togs, I had already pedaled around the Kincheloes' silent pool fifty-one times. Counting made my pre-Ava time pass. To see better, I rode standing up, upper body turned completely poolward. I decided it'd be rude to besiege the Wembleys' home. Chalmers liked me, true, but not that much. I couldn't risk his closing the door while barking, "Sorry, ol' boy. *I* saw her first!" And yet, didn't some of my Ava fascination spring from his inviting tales? Surely that made him a bit responsible for me today?

Finally the Wembleys' yardman, Zeke Jr., appeared, carrying a huge silver tray. (His dad had played the family butler during Chalmers's home-approval trip with Ava decades back.) Now, balancing finger food, under-lit by mirroring silver, Zeke looked uneasy in a starched, white, buttoned jacket.

"It scratchy all right," he admitted as my Schwinn puttered all around his tray of deviled eggs. Two-toned, they looked beautiful as jewelry made for her. "Zeke, I see you need m' help."

"No, sir. I got this easy enough. But it is more stuff coming. You never did see such a fuss as they making. "

"Is she pretty? How much so? Is it what all they say?"

He laughed, shaking his head but keeping that tray dead-level. "Ain't too harsh on the eyes. She a nice size for a woman, but still seem right small for bein' Hollywood. They say she gone upstairs to put on...."

"Bathing suit?"

"Yes, suh. And she don't even sound Yankee. She act right nice. Come in the kitchen, everything. Open the fridge. Be barefoot, too."

"Here, let me get this gate for you, Zeke buddy." He gave me one stern, regretful look, shook his head. "Mr. Chalmers mighty particular today . . ."

"Okay, I know, I know," and rolled off some.

"Zeke would if Zeke could, but today they acting worried 'bout her. Getting looked at and all."

I nodded, recommenced my bike-circling. In ten minutes, mint-green bathing caps showed through slats. I heard one splash then a shout suspiciously husky. One brand-new beach umbrella opened, red and white. Soon Chalmers's most mayoral voice, then squeals from two of his four kids. Pretty Creighton, about to go off the high dive, at last saw me loitering. I had stopped my bike mid-road. My favorite dance partner, guilty of keeping me out, did feebly wave. And behind her right hand, she pointed downward with her left, meaning "She's right *here*." Agony. I signaled back so readily, I half-slipped off my parked bike.

"Creighton, I know you are not waving. Is it a certain movie-mad youngster Zeke warned we might expect? Ignore him," Chalmers said plainly. "He'll go away." But I circled and re-circled like those tigers that round a tree in *Little Black Sambo*. Like them I would risk becoming butter. I already was.

Then I heard a dark laugh new to me, only not. It emerged spiral-shaped. "You try that again, fella, I'll crack you a good one," the voice jokingly told someone lucky.

After all the hours and U-turns, my sunburn grew far hotter. I decided to park in shade, incidentally very near the fence. To steady myself, I leaned closer, and my fingers slid between two boards, and the hand chanced to appear not three feet from Chalmers's silver head. He half-hollered, "For God's sake, ask him over the Berlin Wall but for two minutes. And if he stays, I want his father phoned. Creighton, I distinctly told you, none of your little…"

They sent Zeke Jr. out to lead me in. Head hanging, he acted even more embarrassed than I felt. I was not quite ashamed enough to miss the spectacle of Ava live. Even an Ava cold was an Ava live! Led through the high gate, I told myself not to expect a word from her; no interview; and certainly no signature. It was just the sight of her I craved. I already felt so close to her; I just counted on Ava's kind of recognizing that, you know?

I wore white-soled blue Keds, a terry-top embroidered with red anchors, plus that mature-making blue Jantzen. I just stood there in these. No one offered me a Coke. Nobody looked up from slicking Coppertone across long legs. They all appeared ashamed of me. For me. I tried not to let that register. The world smelled of chlorine, rum, and basil. There were two strange, greasy businessmen wearing suits and dark glasses. There was a woman in a white one-piece standing there against the bright umbrella. "This the kid busted in?" The lady proved quite tall, but her narrow waist made her look smaller, finer. No jewelry. In her right hand, one lucky Lucky Strike put off smoke, in her left hand, a clear drink, its ice clinking. The lady was barefoot, of course, and I could see wet footprints leading to where she expected me. Her weight on one hip, she looked a little tough. Thing is, she was not at all a statue (as in *The Barefoot Contessa* or *One Touch of Venus*). She was just a woman. She had sides. You might walk around her and see the hidden parts not showing screenward. I, squinting in sunlight, tried not to seem her supplicant, but kept approaching nonetheless. (I hoped my mouth was not open. I could not be sure.) She was thirty-five, absolutely poured into that suit, her skin two octaves duskier than Lena Horne's, cheekbones out to here, black hair shining down her back, quite wild. Cherokee blood? Through a smirk or grin, she seemed to take pity on the jerky kid so uninvited but getting through that fortress fence. After drawing one long drag off her smoke (seemed whiter than most), she looked toward the Wembleys. They concentrated on anything but this meeting. So she stared right down at me. Creighton, till this moment one of my best friends, called from her diving board, "He's somebody from my school" With one laugh, the beautiful woman, somehow accidentally my mom's age, acknowledged my crazy baby-bird gaze by picking one piece of tobacco off her tongue. Then, with a sleepy grin, she said quite low, "And whose little boy are *you*?"

A minor seizure rolled in me like theme music. But the Wembleys only chuckled, hearing in her words a veiled put-down. Zeke shook his head, studied fence. And yet I'd heard the sexiest and kindest voice alive, with me its very subject. I'd heard such raw flirtation that it cooked me. I answered the one way I could. In silence. I pointed right toward her, right up to Ava's chest. *Yours. Your little boy is who.* That got a laugh for sure. She made a wry mouth. Chalmers nodded, understood, flung out one party cackle. How might I, voiceless, tell her what she meant to me? How could I explain that she was more beautiful for being willing to come South and let a hick like me monopolize her for even a second? How to explain that she'd inspired me to be—not beautiful, that was hopeless—but something, anything, else?

Suddenly her jaw was moving strangely, swinging up then down, some need independent from her cigarette. Could it be...not, gum? Yes, my God, here came forth quite a pink bubble. Then the bubble popped, she sucked it right up, guileless. She could do anything she liked. She was her, she. And what might a nine-year-old boy have done to/with her, even if finally swimming here alone together? Did I want to *touch* her or *be* her? She turned away while asking, "Like a hard-boiled egg, baby?" Then mute, I aimed Keaton-silent toward the tall gate, using it. No one said good-bye, or come back. Nor did I risk saying thanks. —On my bike sputtering home slow, I stopped behind a huge pyracantha bush, orange berries spread among its own thorns like roe, like gore. And, far from the chance of being overheard, though still in earshot of poolside high-jinks, were those lazy giggles at my expense? I cried. I told myself in the prose of *Modern Screen*, "It never could have worked between us, being, as we are, from Two Different Worlds." But I didn't believe that for a minute. Tears came down in great orgasmic gushes. I coughed out whole emotions that I could not name. Then I noticed an unaccountable erection trapped in the mesh pouch of my suit. I remember looking down at it, birthday candle, inborn torture device barometer. Oh, the loneliness of it, up and all alone two hundred yards from Ava Gardner.

She had admired my persistence in getting to her. But maybe distance was what I had most needed? Maybe that's what I bought tickets to? Here I thought I was in love with a former local, but her astronomical comparisons were what thrilled me most. I went into the darkness for our intimacy; but I weighed sixty pounds, and she was made of fire and light, her face shown house-sized.

Just now, in noon sun, she'd gleamed, a stunning mammal, almost studly in her confident naturalness and flat force, and yet…she was already en route to forty. Ava had somehow slipped up and let me see her out of makeup and off duty, a civilian. She was stupidly living in regular-time and getting a little too tanned and eating paprikaed eggs and stimulating herself via smoke and booze and Bazooka gum and being somehow too visibly, promiscuously…human. My God, what a lapse. Crushing, that. The girl needed direction.

I aimed home admitting it had been real, real awkward beside the Wembleys' borrowed pool. Breaking in on a movie star party felt more embarrassing than I've even let myself hint here. Pedaling, listless, to my house, saddened yet enlarged, I found my inner thighs chafed red, blistered from all those hours spent circling Ava by bike.

It would take me months to win back the Wembleys. But considering how much Chalmers and his Eva drank, they tended to forget things faster than most. My stalking Ava had been a very brave and pushy thing to try. And it had only made me sad, her sadder, everybody. Now I understood: it was just a job, being Ava. Her job, our joy. But, whatever the cost to either of us, I'd seen her. At age nine, I had got my body to her body. And now I saw, it was not that, not about just that, alas. It had very little to do with a body, anyone's. And yet, you know? Forty-three years later, I cannot begin to say how glad I am I risked all that.

NOW THAT YOU'RE INITIATED, you really must visit Smithfield's Ava Gardner Museum, okay? (325 East Market. The phone number is 919-934-5830. Or try www. avagardner.org.) It's even open two to five each Sunday, after church. Another man, mad for her, set it up till, in the museum itself, he had a stroke that killed him young. In sight of all her posters, the clothes she wore in her best-known films.

WHAT, FINALLY, ARE MOVIE STARS for? Maybe to prove that Desire, writ large up there, is probably the best we'll ever get of Wisdom. To show us how, happier, we might've looked. To make us pay such major money for mere Junior Mints. Stars are meant to keep us from going to bed at 8 p.m., sobbing. Movie stars "stand for us" when we know we were born kneeling and will die crawling on our bellies like reptiles. Movie stars are what we tithe to, wank to, dress like, wish for, doubt would really like us. They are what we would all die for, given the slightest chance. Movie stars cannot often be from around here, since they're mostly compared to heavenly bodies. But some few have it both ways. They are up there glittering on high but with their shoes kicked off. And they still look pretty great from underneath. Movie stars are those most not us, who still *are*.

Our Princess of the Luckless never let her local membership lapse. That's why we still protect her hereabouts. She always stayed somebody decent's daughter, sister, former fiancée. Born with nothing, she turned out to be a gentleman, Ava.

That's why—like Chalmers Wembley IV—all of us who grew up around here, we've really spent our lives in love with someone extra. And, however catholic my well-known bachelor tastes, however improbable this connection might sound to some, it is true: I have always been engaged to Ava Gardner.

I'm still saving myself.

I just turned fifty-four years old.

Somehow I live alone now.

I remember her daily.

And—if not the goddess's—whose little boy am I?

Margaret Atwood

Ava Gardner Reincarnated as a Magnolia

Somehow I've never succeeded
in being taken seriously. They made me
wear things that were ruffled: off-the-
shoulder blouses, the tiered skirts
of flouncing Spanish dancers, though I never
quite got the hauteur—I was always tempted
to wink, show instead of tragic
outstretched neck, a slice of flank. Now look
at me: a vaginal hot pink,
vibrant as a laxative bottle—
not, given the company, a respectable
colour. Let's face it: when I was in
the flesh, to be beautiful and to be
a woman was a kind
of joke. The men waited to nail
me in the trophy room, on the pool-
table if possible, the women simply to poke
my eyes out. Me, I would have preferred
to enjoy myself—a little careless
love, some laughs, a few drinks—but that was not an option.

What would have given
me weight? Substance? For them.
Long canines? Vengeance?
A stiletto hidden in my skirt,
a greyish rainbow of fate
like an aureole of rancid lard—
or better: dress up in armour,
ride across the steppes, leading a horde
of armed murderers. That gets you a statue,

copper or stone, with a lofty frown
—jaw clenched as if chewing—
like those erected by the sober
citizens years later,
for all the sad destroyers.

Well, to hell with them. I'd rather
be a flower, even this one, so much like
a toilet-paper decoration
at a high school dance.
Even that, to be trampled
underfoot next day by the janitor
sweeping up, even the damp flirtation,
the crumpled tulle, even the botched smooch
in the parking lot, the boy with the fat neck
and the hip flask, even the awkward fumbling
with the weird bodice, cheap perfume between
the freckled breasts, would have been better
than all their history, the smudged
flags, dry parchments, layers of dead bone
they find so solemn, the slaughters
they like to memorize, and tell
their children also to pray to

here, where they hate bouquets, the pleasures
of thoughtless botany, a glass
of wine or two on the terrace,
bare leg against white trouser
under the table, that ancient ploy
and vital puzzle, water-
of-life cliché that keeps things going,
tawdry and priceless, the breeze
that riffles through what now
may be my leaves, my green closed
eyes, my negligible
vulgar fragile incandescent petals,
these many mouths, lipsticked and showy
and humid as kisses opening

in a hot house, oh I'd give anything
to have it back again, in
the flesh, the flesh,
which was all the time
I ever had for anything. The joy.

Robert Graves

Not to Sleep

Not to sleep all the night long, for pure joy,
Counting no sheep and careless of chimes
Welcoming the dawn confabulation
Of birch, her children, who discuss idly
Fanciful details of the promised coming—
Will she be wearing red, or russet, or blue,
Or pure white?—whatever she wears, glorious:
Not to sleep all the night long, for pure joy,
This is given to few but at last to me,
So that when I laugh and stretch and leap from bed
I shall glide downstairs, my feet brushing the carpet
In courtesy to civilized progression,
Though, did I wish, I could soar through the open window
And perch on a branch above, acceptable ally
Of the birds still alert, grumbling gently together.

Select Ava Gardner Filmography

The Killers, 1946
One Touch of Venus, 1948
Pandora and the Flying Dutchman, 1951
Show Boat, 1951
The Snows of Kilimanjaro, 1952
Mogambo, 1953
The Barefoot Contessa, 1954
Bhowani Junction, 1956
The Little Hut, 1957
The Sun Also Rises, 1957
On the Beach, 1959
The Night of the Iguana, 1964
Seven Days in May, 1964
The Bible: In the Beginning, 1966
The Life and Times of Judge Roy Bean, 1972
Earthquake, 1974

Notes

Page xxii
She also inspired at least two jazz compositions, Shaw and Harding's 1945 "The Grabtown Grapple," recorded by The Gramercy Five, and Martin Eagle's 2004 "Ava Gardner."

An apocryphal story about Sinatra's March 1951 recording of "I'm a Fool to Want You" has the singer running out of the studio in tears, so tortured was he by his love of Ava. He and Ava would be married by year's end.

Ava would star in three films based on Hemingway works: "The Killers" (1946), "Snows of Kilimanjaro" (1952), and *The Sun also Rises* (1957).

Page 38
"Working at Pam-Pam's" is a double-helix abecedarian, which entwines two alphabets—one at the beginning of the line and one at the end.

Page 56
On the Beach is a novel by Nevil Shute about nuclear holocaust upon which the 1959 film, starring Ava Gardner, Gregory Peck, Fred Astaire, and Anthony Perkins was based.

Page 125
In her autobiography, *Ava: My Story*, the actress discusses two terminated pregnancies while married to Sinatra (184-187).

Pages 127, 129
These lyrics were inspired by a passage in Lee Server's 2006 biography, *Ava Gardner: Love is Nothing*: "'We never fought in bed,' Ava would tell friends. 'The fight would start on the way to the bidet.' The 'love nest' in the Pacific Palisades

became the neighborhood tinderbox, ever ready to explode with the newlyweds' raging disagreements" (245).

Page 145
"Ava (a nod to a famed beauty)" was inspired by a reference in the actress' autobiography to a phone call to Stuart Granger, who had co-starred with her in *Bhowani Junction* and *The Little Hut* (Server 492).

Page 189
"Not to Sleep," while not written specifically for the actress, was a gift to Ava from the poet.

Works Cited

Gardner, Ava. *Ava: My Story*. New York: Bantam, 1990.
Server, Lee. *Ava Gardner: Love is Nothing*. New York:
  St. Martin's Press, 2006.

Contributors

Derek Adams was born in London, England in 1957. He is a professional photographer, whose poems have been widely published in magazines. He has published three collections of poems: *Postcards to Olympus, Everyday Objects, Chance Remarks* and *Unconcerned but Not Indifferent*. He was the BBC Wildlife Poet of the Year 2006.

Al Alvarez is a poet, novelist, literary critic, anthologist, and author of many highly praised non-fiction books on topics ranging from suicide, divorce and dreams, to poker, North Sea oil, and mountaineering. His most recent books are *New and Selected Poems, The Writer's Voice,* and *Risky Business*.

Margaret Atwood, throughout her thirty-five years of writing, has received numerous awards and many honorary degrees. She is the author of more than thirty-five volumes of poetry, fiction, and nonfiction and is perhaps best known for her novels, which include *The Edible Woman* (1970), *The Handmaid's Tale* (1983), and *The Blind Assassin*, which won the prestigious Booker Prize in 2000.

Rob Berretta is a singer/songwriter from New York City. A graduate of Wesleyan University, he works as a performing arts agent and performs in clubs around the Northeast. His album *Songs from the Big Martin* is available at CDBaby. com.

Blue Tatoo is the *nom de plume* of Tammy Turner Peaden, a paramedic from Tarboro, NC. Emergency Medicine is her job. Poetry is her passion.

Peg Boyers is Executive Editor of *Salmagundi* magazine and teaches poetry at Skidmore College. She is author of *Hard Bread and Honey with Tobacco*.

Ian Rosales Casocot teaches in Silliman University in the Philippines. He edited *FutureShock Prose: An Anthology of Young Filipino Writers* in 2002, and published his first short story collection *Old Movies and Other Stories* in 2006. He has won several literary awards in his country.

Mario Cabré (1916-1990), a *torero* who turned to acting in the 1940s, appeared in several films including *Pandora and the Flying Dutchman* (1951) with Ava and James Mason.

Cheryl Clarke is the Director of the Office of Diverse Community Affairs and LGBT Concerns and a member of the graduate faculty of of the Department of Women and Gender Studies at Rutgers University, New Brunswick campus. She is the author of four books of poetry since 1983: *Narratives: Poems In The Tradition Of Black Women*, *Living As A Lesbian*, *Humid Pitch*, and *Experimental Love*. Her poetry and prose have appeared in numerous publications.

William Corbett is the Director, Student Writing Activities/ Lecturer in the MIT Program in Writing and Humanistic Studies. He edits the small press Pressed Wafer and runs the literary program at CUE Art Foundation, a non-profit gallery in New York City's Chelsea.

Joseph Donahue is the author of a number of poetry collections, including *Before Creation*, *Monitions of the Approach*, *World Well Broken*, *Terra Lucida*, and *Incidental Eclipse*, of which John Ashbery has written, "This sequence confirms Donahue as one of the major American poets of this time."

Cathryn Essinger's first book, *A Desk in the Elephant House*, won the Walt McDonald First Book Award, from Texas Tech UP. Her poems have been anthologized in *The Poetry An-*

thology, 1912-2002; Poetry Daily: 366 poems; O Taste and See: Food Poems, and *Grrrrr: A Collection of Poems About Bears*. She teaches writing classes at Edison Community College in Piqua, Ohio.

Clive Fencott is a senior lecturer in the School of Computing at the University of Teesside in the North East of England. He researches and lectures in the design of computer games and Virtual Environments (VEs) in general.

Roxanne Fontana is a singer, songwriter and musician who has released two cds. Roxanne's talents include fashion design and astrology, and she has penned a memoir, *American Girl*. Roxanne spent five years in the 90's living in Times Square in a building that was an infamous hang out of the young Sinatra.

Susan Gilmore is an Associate Professor of American Literature and Women's, Gender, and Sexuality Studies at Central Connecticut State University. She received her M.F.A. in poetry from Cornell University. She loves musicals, skates badly, and remembers many warm Decembers in Ottawa with Alan and Anne, to whom she dedicates her poem.

Pere Gimferrer has long been one of the most prestigious Catalan writers. His poetic work has been distinguished with the most prestigious Catalan and Spanish awards. He is a member of the Spanish Royal Academy of Language and of the Royal Academy of *Belles Lletres* of Barcelona. Awards received include the Ramon Llull Award (1983), the National Literature Award (1988) and the National Spanish Arts Award (1998).

Robert Graves, a poet, classical scholar, novelist, and critic, was one of the greatest writers of the 20th Century. Athough he produced over 100 books he is perhaps best known for the novel *I, Claudius* (1934), *The White Goddess* (1948) and *Greek Myths* (1955). Robert Graves died in 1985 in Deja, the Majorcan village he had made his home since 1929.

Daniel Gula, a 2004 Nimrod Pablo Neruda Poetry Contest Finalist, has numerous publications to his credit, including an essay in *Reflections, the United Nations Literary Review.*

Allan Gurganus's first published story "Minor Heroism" appeared in the *New Yorker* when he was twenty six. A 2006 Guggenheim Fellow, he is the award-winning author of the novel *Oldest Living Confederate Widow Tells All*, the CBS adaptation of which won four Emmy awards. His novella, *Blessed Assurance*, has become part of the Harvard Business School's Ethics curriculum. His published works include *White People, Plays Well With Others*, and *The Practical Heart: Four Novellas*. His short fiction appears in the *New Yorker, Harper's*, and other magazines.

Barbara Hamby is the author of three books of poetry: *Delirium, The Alphabet of Desire*, and *Babel*, which won the AWP/Donald Hall Prize. She teaches in the creative writing program at Florida State University.

Michael S. Harper, University Professor and professor of English at Brown University, is the author of numerous volumes of poetry including *Songlines in Michaeltree, Honorable Amendments, Images of Kin*, and *History is Your Own Heartbeat*. He has been honored with the Frost Medal and the Melville Cane Award from the Poetry Society of America, and the Black Academy of Arts and Letters Award, among others.

Jim Harrison's poetry collections include *Plain Song* (1965), *Locations* (1968), *Walking* (1967), and *Outlyer and Ghazals* (1969). His novels and novellas include *Wolf* (1971), *Legends of the Fall* (1979), *Sundog* (1984), *Dalva* (1988), and *Julip* (1994).

Yorgos Ioannou (1927-1985) published his first collection of poetry in 1954 and, a decade later, his first important collection of prose appeared. Though he continued his teaching career, he was henceforth primarily a writer, producing stories, articles, literary criticism, translations and a variety of short prose works.

Walker Joe Jackson has written 15 books and a few poems. He is a retired engineer living in Central Florida with his two Affenpinschers.

Jarret Keene is author of the poetry collections *Monster Fashion* and *A Boy's Guide to Arson* and the unauthorized rock-band bio *The Killers: Destiny Is Calling Me*. He has edited several books, including *The Underground Guide to Las Vegas, Neon Crush*, and *Las Vegas Noir*.

Lynda Kenny is a housewife and mother who lives just outside Belfast in Northern Ireland. A member of a small online writing community, www.morewriting.co.uk, she also has had published a compilation called *The Eve Project* and most recently in a book devoted to micro stories called *Wonderful World of Worders*.

Cheryl Diane Kidder's fiction and poetry have appeared in *The Reed, Amelia, Dog River Review, Alchemy, Sandscript, Insolent Rudder, August Cutter, Three Candles, Outsider Ink* and the *Clackamas Literary Review*, and *Write From Life*.

David Kirby teaches is the Robert O. Lawton Distinguished Professor of English at Florida State University. *The House on Boulevard St.: New and Selected Poems* was a National Book Award Finalist in 2007. His latest collection is *The Temple Gate Called Beautiful*.

Steve Kistulentz's work has appeared in the *Antioch, Black Warrior, Crab Orchard* and *New England Reviews, Caesura, New Letters, Quarterly West,* and many others. He is a two-time winner of the John Mackay Shaw Academy of American Poets Prize, and was recently selected by Mark Strand to appear in *Best New Poets 2008*.

Paloma LaPuerta is a Professor of Spanish at Central Connecticut State University and specializes in 20th-century Spanish poetry. **Ninon Larché** is a freelance translator and interpreter living in Durban, South Africa. She also teaches and does research in the field of Translation Studies.

Julia Lisella is the author of two collections of poetry, *Terrain* and *Love Song Hiroshima*, a chapbook, and is Assistant Professor of English at Regis College in Weston, Massachusetts. You can learn more about her poetry and scholarship at www. julialisella.com.

David Lloyd directs the Creative Writing Program at Le Moyne College. In 2009 New American Press published *The Gospel According to Frank*. His other publications include *Boys: Stories and a Novella*, *The Urgency of Identity: Contemporary English-language Poetry from Wales,* and *Writing on the Edge: Interviews with Writers and Editors of Wales*. His writing has appeared in numerous magazines, including *Colorado Review, Crab Orchard Review,* and *Denver Quarterly.* In 2000, he received the Poetry Society of America's Robert H. Winner Memorial Award.

Clarence Major, a prize-winning poet, painter and novelist, is the author of ten books of poetry, including *Configurations: New and Selected Poems 1958-1998*, a National Book Award Bronze Medal finalist, and *Myself Painting*.

Peter Mackridge is Emeritus Professor of Modern Greek at Oxford University and the author of several books on Modern Greek language and literature. **Jackie Willcox** has recently retired as librarian of the Russian and Eurasian Studies Centre at St Antony's College, Oxford. She has published two volumes of Katerina Anghelaki-Rooke's poetry in English.

Leo Luke Marcello is the author of *Nothing Grows Forever in One Place: Poems of a Sicilian American, The Secret Proximity of Everywhere, Blackrobe's Love Letters*, and *Silent Film*. He edited and published *Everything Comes to Light: A Festschrift for Joy Scantlebury*. His awards include two Shearman Fellowships, a Shearman Endowed Professorship, and a grant from the

Louisiana Endowment for the Humanities. He passed away in 2005, after an eighteen-month battle with GBM, a malignant brain cancer.

Margaret Meyers teaches in the MA in Writing Program at Johns Hopkins University. Her essay, "A Bend in Which River," was included in the *Best American Essays, 1998*. Her other articles and fiction have been published in *Shenandoah, Sewanee Magazine*, and *Philosophy Today. Swimming in the Congo*, a book inspired by her experiences as a missionary's child, was named a Book of the Year by the New York Public Library.

David Miller graduate from the University of Virginia in 1992 with an M.F.A. in poetry. His poems and photographs have appeared in *Callaloo* and *The Poet*.

Lyndon Morgans is the singer and songwriter with the Welsh folk-noir band Songdog: they have released four albums, *The Way Of The World, Haiku, The Time Of Summer Lightning*, and *A Wretched Sinner's Song*. Morgans also received the Verity Bargate award for his play *Water Music*. www.songdog.co.uk

Michael O'Leary was born in 1950 in Auckland, New Zealand. He is the author of five novels, including a trilogy. Also, he has published about ten volumes of poetry. Under his imprint The Earl of Seacliff Art Workshop (www.earlofseacliff.co.nz) he has published many New Zealand writers.

Antony Owen, the author of *My Father's Eyes Were Blue*, is from Allesley, Coventry, and has been writing poetry for fifiteen years.

Laurence Petit, a Maître de Conférences in the English Department of Université Paul Valéry-Montpellier 3, France, has published articles on text and image in contemporary British fiction, as well as translations of essays by George Bataille and Pierre Bourdieu. She is co-editor of Poetics of the Iconotext, a translation of two major studies by Liliane Louvel, and co-translator of A.S. Byatt's latest novel, The Children's Book, with **Pascal Bataillard**, a Maître de Conférences in the English Department of Université Lyon-Lumière 2, France. He has published numerous articles on James Joyce and 20th-century fiction, with a particular focus on psychoanalytical theory. He was a member of the team who produced the 2004 Gallimard translation into French of *Ulysses*.

Alton Rivers spent twenty-one years in the U.S. Air Force, which took him from the Vietnam War to the American Embassy in London. Since retiring, he has worked in city management. He lives with his wife, Conni, on Grand Lake in Oklahoma.

Robert Rodriguez is a film director and screenwriter whose credits include "Planet Terror" from *Grindhouse, The Adventures of Sharkboy and Lava Girl, Sin City, Spy Kids I, II,* and *III,* and *Shorts*.

Charles Rossiter writes, performs, and promotes poetry. www. Poetrypoetry.com is the latest in a long list of poetry projects that include the creating and hosting the *Poetry Motel*, a cable television program still seen in upstate New York and neighboring states, and organizing all-day poetry readings at the Washington Monument. He received an NEA Fellowship for poetry and has been nominated for a Pushcart Prize.

Tom Russell has recorded one DVD and 20 albums of original material. His songs have been recorded by Johnny Cash, Nanci Griffith, Doug Sahm, Dave Alvin, Joe Ely, Ian Tyson, and others and have appeared in a dozen films including *Songcatcher* and *Tremors*.

Lynn Veach Sadler, a former college president, has published widely in academics and creative writing . One story appears in Del Sol's *Best of 2004 Butler Prize Anthology*; another won the 2006 Abroad Writers Contest/Fellowship (France). *Not Your Average Poet (on Robert Frost)* was a Pinter Review Prize for Drama Silver Medalist in 2005.

Pia Savage is a fourth generation New Yorker who truly loves Manhattan. She lived there since the 70's but recently moved to South Carolina. Her blog, CourtingDestiny.com, contains personal essays and fiction.

Vivian Shipley is the Connecticut State University Distinguished Professor from Southern Connecticut State University. Her seventh book of poems, *Hardboot: Poems New & Old* won the 2006 Paterson Prize for Sustained Literary Achievement. She has won the Hackney Literary Award for Poetry from Birmingham-Southern University in Alabama and the New Millennium Poetry Prize.

Kirpal Singh, published worldwide for over 30 years, is a renowned poet, fictionist, and scholar. He has performed at many major arts festivals, including Edinburgh, Cambridge, Toronto, and York, and his poems have been dramatized Off Broadway. In 1997, he was the Distinguished International Writer at the Iowa Writers' Workshop. He is the author of *Thinking Hats and Coloured Turbans: Creativity Across Cultures*.

Alain Souchon is a French singer, songwriter, and actor. He has released 15 albums and played roles in seven films. He wrote the theme for Francois Truffaut's 1979 film *Love on the Run*.

Virgil Suarez was born in Havana, Cuba, in 1962 and has lived in the United States since 1974. In addition to his seven collections of poetry (most recently *90 Miles*), he is the author of four novels, a collection of stories, and two memoirs. He also has edited many successful anthologies. He lives in Florida.

Katherine Sugg is an Associate Professor of English and coordinator of Latino Studies at Central Connecticut State University. She is the author of *Gender and Allegory in Transamerican Fiction and Performance*.

Suzanne Vega is a singer and songwriter, whose albums include *Suzanne Vega*, *Solitude Standing*, *Days of Open Hand*, and *Beauty and Crime*.

Ben Vaughn is a singer/songwriter who has recorded several albums, scored several films, and provided award-winning music for more than a dozen TV shows and pilots, including *Third Rock from the Sun* and *That 70s Show*. He also created *Rambler '65*, a much-publicized album recorded entirely in his car.

John Williams was born in 1945 in Liverpool England and was variously a tailor, sailor and teacher. He has survived Beatlemania, Loons and post-modern sarcasm.

Briar Wood grew up in Auckland, New Zealand and now lives in London where she works as a lecturer in Creative Writing and English Literature. Her poetry has been widely published.

Gail Wronsky is the author or coauthor of seven books including *Again the Gemini are in the Orchard*, *Dying for Beauty*, and *Volando Bajito*, as translator. She is Director of Creative Writing and Syntext at Loyola Marymount University in Los Angeles. She is a regular instructor in the Prague Summer Program, Western Michigan University.

Acknowledgements

All works used by permission.

"America – Whore of Babylon – Mars, Mars, Mars" from www.vivafontana1959.com
"American Drag Rhapsody: J. Edgar Hoover in Havana" from *Guide to the Blue Tongue*: Poems by Virgil Suarez. Used with permission of the poet and University of Illinois Press.
"Ava (a nod to a famed beauty)" first appeared at www.morewriting.co.uk
"Ava Gardner" first appeared at www.poetrycritical.net
"Ava Gardner Blues." Words and music by Ben Vaughn. published by Quonset Music / Admin. by Bug Music (BI)
"The Ava Gardner House" first appeared at www.nthposition.com
"Ava Gardner: Queen of Earthquakes" was originally published in *South Carolina Review* 33. 2 (Spring 2001) and was included in *Monster Fashion* (Manic D Press 2004).
"Ava Gardner Reincarnated as a Magnolia," from *MORNING IN THE BURNED HOUSE* by Margaret Atwood. Copyright © 1995 by Margaret Atwood. Reprinted by permission of Houghton Mifflin Harcourt Publishing Company. All rights reserved.
"Ava Gardner Shades the Grave of Gregory Peck" first appeared at www.copperfieldreview.com
"La Beauté D'Ava Gardner" by Alain Souchon from *Ultra Moderne* © 1988 Virgin France SA.
"Becoming a Servant to the Stars" first appeared at ttp://www.scm.tees.ac.uk/p.c.fencott/
"Carrying a Torch (The Usher's Song)" first appeared at www.liverpooltales.com/
"Channeling Ava Gardner" first appeared at www.courtingdestiny.com
"Cirque du Liz and Dick (Puerto Vallarta)" appeared in *Poems for Infidels*, Red Hen Press (2005) and also in Runes (2005)